I

i i i i i i

!NNOVATION

!NNOVATION

How innovators think, act and change our world

Kim Chandler McDonald

KoganPage

LONDON PHILADELPHIA NEW DELHI

First published in Great Britain and the United States in 2013 by Kogan Page Limited

2nd Floor, 45 Gee Street
London EC1V 3RS
United Kingdom
www.koganpage.com

1518 Walnut Street, Suite 1100
Philadelphia PA 19102
USA

4737/23 Ansari Road
Daryaganj
New Delhi 110002
India

© Kim Chandler McDonald, 2013

The right of Kim Chandler McDonald to be identified as the author of this work has been asserted by her in accordance with the Copyright, Designs and Patents Act 1988.

ISBN   978 0 7494 6966 5
E-ISBN   978 0 7494 6967 2

British Library Cataloguing-in-Publication Data

A CIP record for this book is available from the British Library.

Library of Congress Cataloging-in-Publication Data

McDonald, Kim Chandler.
    Innovation : how world-class innovators rock their roles / Kim Chandler McDonald.
       pages cm
    ISBN 978-0-7494-6966-5 (pbk.) – ISBN 978-0-7494-6967-2 ( )   1. Creative ability in business.
2. Success in business.   3. Technological innovations.   4. Organizational change.   I. Title.
    HD53.M379 2013
    658.4'063–dc23
                                                                                                          2013020944

Typeset by Graphicraft Limited, Hong Kong
Printed and bound in India by Replika Press Pvt Ltd

*For Michael
Most.*

We are like dwarfs on the shoulders of giants,
so that we can see more than they....
                    Bernard of Chartres [12th century]

There's a way of playing safe, there's a way of
using tricks and there's the way I like to play,
which is dangerously, where you're going to take
a chance on making mistakes in order to create
something you haven't created before.
                                    Dave Brubeck

The theory of relativity occurred to me by
intuition, and music is the driving force behind
this intuition... My new discovery is the result of
musical perception.
                                    Albert Einstein

CONTENTS

ACKNOWLEDGEMENTS

Thanks to:

Michael – for everything.

The McDonalds for sharing their farm and their family with me.

Marco Del Vecchio who was the first to suggest that not only should this book be written, but that I should be the one to write it.

Andy Rotman-Zaod and Julian Keith Loren for the introductions they made and their faith that I would live up to their effusiveness.

Donna DuCarme, Diane Macey, Jason Revere, Russell Watson, Tracey Gibson and Agnes Benjamin for being bothered to stay close, even while far away – and Carl Lewis who knows he doesn't have to.

Linda Tolbert and Simon Kearns for their energy, enthusiasm and extraordinariness.

Shelby Piton for knowing where it's all buried and guarding the shovel.

Liz Gooster for taking a chance.

All the !nnovators, and their teams, for their inspiration, their insight, their generosity of spirit and their graciousness in putting up with a pestering author such as myself.

To all of these wonderful people I owe at least a glass of wine (though a few may have to wait a couple of years before they're legally old enough to drink it). Some of them I owe a winery... I'll see what I can do!

ABOUT THE AUTHOR

Kim Chandler McDonald is Executive Vice President of KimmiC, a company she co-founded with her husband Michael, which specializes in adaptive approaches, robust technologies and leading edge innovations. A thought leader, sought after speaker and advisory board member, Kim is an advocate for disruptive approaches and transformational trends such as Flat World Navigation, meHealth and empowered endusers.

Kim has built and maintains a far-reaching network of global thought leaders. As the world's first, branded, Flat World Navigator, Kim was included in the inaugural 'LinkedIn Power Profiles – Australia' list of 2012. Formerly, Kim was immersed in media as a writer and editor for national and international newspapers and magazines as well as being one of the host/producers of the award winning English Breakfast radio show. Kim specializes in interviewing international thought leaders and influencers – in particular those who she'd like to share a bottle of bubbles with.

She loves chocolate, champagne and beer – but not together – usually...

The orchestration of innovation

Three core axioms infuse this book: 1) innovation drives change – cultural, societal and economic; 2) innovation, in some form, touches each and every one of us, wherever we may be, as individuals, communities and societies as a whole; and 3) innovators deserve recognition, celebration and applause. This book is my hands clapping. I hope, by the end of our time together, you join me in my ovation.

I am taking you on a journey around the world. On the way I will introduce you to innovators who have broken the mould, led the pack, and moved their own particular mountains in fields as diverse as business and technology, engineering and education, government and social policy, media, medicine and more. While they are as diverse as any other group – as are the areas from which they draw inspiration – there are traits that link many, if not most of them.

Though at times it may be daunting, innovators are compelled to tell their truths – whether we, the public want to hear them or not. Some boldly go where no one has been, or thought to be, before. Most of them are applauded for it, but that is not why they do what they do. Innovators run when most are content to walk; this is true even when their leaps of faith can leave some of us queasy with anxiety. Without their willingness to delve into the depths of the unknown, we would all be lessened; their innovations have changed the way we see, and live in, our world.

Think where we might be if Michael Faraday hadn't brought us the innovation of electromagnetism, or Nikola Tesla the alternating current. Niels Bohr's work with quantum mechanics is the basis for all we take for granted in communication and modern electronics. Perhaps my favourite historical innovator is Johannes Gutenberg, he of the precious printing press. His work, which brought books to the masses, led to reformations in religion, politics and society as a whole.

Looking forward, innovation will be as important in our next 'great leap forward' as it was during the Industrial Revolution. Without the steam engine and Spinning Jenny, our world economy would look much different. In all likelihood the same can be said for those innovations that are now, or will soon be, presenting themselves. It is these innovations that will ensure that we survive and, with any luck, thrive in the new Global Digital Economy (GDE) – and it is innovators that we have to thank for this.

Together, we're going to find out what makes innovators tick, talk and tremble. Perhaps, by understanding these things, we will be able to understand the future that awaits us all a little more comfortably. In the interviews in this book you'll find answers from artists and authors, engineers and entrepreneurs, doctors and designers, educators and architects, scientists and explorers of space, business people, bankers, politicians, printers, and many more. There are those who focus on the micro, the macro, the profit, the public, the bold, the beautiful, the richest, the poorest, the sun, the moon, the earth, and almost everything in between. There are no right or wrong answers in this book: there is only the exploration and the celebration of innovation and of how these world-class innovators rock their roles.

In travelling through *!nnovation* you also have an opportunity to explore your own innovative thinking. I begin each chapter with a 'word cloud'. Look out for these words as you read each interview. They are the commonalities – the themes, if you will – that link and lead. They are the warp and weft, the contexts and concepts, the melodies and harmonies of this symphony of extraordinary, and extraordinarily innovative, individuals.

Following each main interview I have included a simple 'Keyword imagination exercise'. Take five minutes, close your eyes, and see what thoughts and ideas they inspire. Take some time – some *you* time – to allow your mind to wander freely and make an 'innovation investment' in yourself. There are no right or wrong answers, no test to study for – this is your time to delve into the deep insights shared in these interviews, investigate your own connection to innovation and explore the potential differentiation that you can bring to your world, your business and yourself.

The me-conomics of the GDE

01

Innovating from the e-conomy to the me-conomy

> Agile, Audacity,
> Change, Collaborate,
> Communication, Competition,
> Consumer, Differentiate, Digital,
> Disruptive, Empower, Entrepreneur, Fear,
> Global, Infrastructure, Interaction, Majority, Mobile,
> Revolution, Risk, Tool, Trust, User, Value, World

We are in the midst of an unprecedented time of change and upheaval. It is, therefore, a time of fantastic opportunity for those who act decisively and bravely, and a graveyard for those who do not. The world is changing irrevocably due to three major influences and innovations in the business arena – some incremental, all insistent. First: the era of the engaged and empowered enduser is here. With their ever-increasing expectations, this 'innovation of the individual' is underlining the 'me' in me-conomics and the me-conomy. Second: endusers are becoming ever more aware of the value of their data, and their right to own and control it. Third: mobile, agile businesses in the Global Digital Economy (GDE)/me-conomy are encompassing an ever flattening world.

The most tragic mistakes one could make are: a) believing that it is business as usual; and b) that the ascendancy of the West is irrevoc-able. That notwithstanding, we're going to see opportunities and markets explode exponentially, in both geography and dimensions, as the inhabitants of the 'Majority World' – where the majority of the world's population lives – not only come online but become avid competitors, not just consumers. It is an exciting frontier that is ever more impossible to opt out of. With that in mind, let's look at these issues of innovation in more detail.

In the late 15th century the Gutenberg Press was an innovation that began a societal revolution. It removed the need for cloistered experts – the technocrats of their time – by disseminating the printed word and democratizing knowledge, leading to what could be described as the glimmers of what would eventually become a knowledge-based economy.

Another 'Gutenberg-esque' revolutionary innovation is upon us, and is being made manifest by the transformational technologies enabling enduser empowerment. It is distinguishing itself in various ways, perhaps most importantly in underlining the power of the economies of attention and information/data ownership – founda-tional pillars of the me-conomy and me-conomics, which put indi-viduals, rather than institutions, at the heart of the GDE.

The new GDE/me-conomy is about more than 'deets on Tweets' and Facebook pages, which are simply messaging platforms tuned to trawl users' data. Rather than transformational, these platforms are transitional steps in the evolution of me-conomics. They lack the depth and breadth of functionality to fully embrace and support the needs of the new, knowledge-based GDE. To thrive, rather than just survive in this milieu, collaboration will be a necessity for businesses of any size – this equates to selectively sharing both knowledge and data. Undoubtedly, data has commercial sensitivity and value. As such, businesses will need tools that enable simple, extremely secure cooperation and collaboration at a micro and macro level – by employees, suppliers, channel partners, consumers or customers – to do deals and make money in a far more dynamic way than has ever been seen before.

Another hallmark of successful companies in the GDE/me-conomy will be an understanding that, beyond social networking, they need to create and maintain thriving business communities. These communities are at the heart of this opportunity for the evolution of social platforms and the spread of their influence. And evolve they must, along with their business models, in this era of the empowered enduser.

Endusers have been, and will continue to be, more and more discerning about what content is relevant to them. As 'push' sales campaigns become more and more irrelevant, and fall on increasingly deaf ears, innovations such as the semantic web, Web 3.0 and social media will come to the fore. Alone, none of these innovations is a complete solution. However, when these tools are used effectively together they can empower businesses to engage in democratized, holistic, marketplace-based, two-way relationships that encapsulate the business offerings that consumers/endusers understand and value. These offerings will entail individually targeted materials and messages that drive engagement and deliver personalized services to endusers who are going to demand micro-pitches and requests that are focused purely on their personalized, customized wants and needs. The organizations prepared for this change in the balance of power will effectively enhance and expand the relationship between their business and their communities – and the empowered endusers within them.

The advantages of this new type of relationship are myriad, and go far beyond sales figures. However, they do take work and they involve the evolution of ROI, in as much as no longer will ROI mean 'Return On Investment': in the me-conomy it will equate to 'Return

On Involvement'; and the judicious use of innovative tools such as semantic web, Web 3.0 and social media will enable the creation and maintenance of a meaningful dialogue between all parties. These innovative tools do more than create a medium for businesses to learn more about, and from, the endusers within their communities – and in doing so, create productive, high touch, high value networks, which will be the cornerstone of enduser engagement, which everyone is looking for. They also enable the empowered endusers to find, refine, define, share, manipulate and mesh information – in particular their own information.

Current business models find many organizations, some more obviously than others, 'borrowing' enduser data and profiting from it. To my mind, this situation is not unlike allowing a random stranger to walk into your home, rummage through your drawers, read your diary to find out what your likes and dislikes are, and then sell you items they think will appeal to you. For many companies, their current business models are dependent upon such borrowing continuing. Yet, I posit that it will not continue in its current state for much longer, as the new GDE and me-conomy marketplace matures.

It will not be long before endusers grasp that their data is *their* intellectual property. Empowered by the innovative evolution of authentication and authorization tools, they will be able to decide when, where and with whom their information is shared – or if it is shared at all. This could result in the cessation of 'phishing' communications, a reduction in internet predators, cyber-bullying and identity theft. Data and knowledge, already acknowledged to be valuable, may become a unit of currency in and of itself and be traded as such – perhaps in a 'marketplace of ideas'. It is not a huge leap to suppose that businesses, currently ensconced in the 'borrowing business model', may be forced – either by policy or by the increasing me-conomic acumen of endusers – to share the revenue they make from using this data.

With innovative tools, techniques and technologies empowering engaged endusers, the me-conomy is quickly becoming a central pillar of a flattening world's GDE. As such, it is not just 'the borrowers of data' who must rethink their business models. Be it by restructure, redesign or reduction, the bastion of business as bricks, rather than clicks, has forever changed – an online presence is not just the norm, it is an undeniable necessity.

The mobile, online market is, increasingly, a major driver of national economies and employment. The changes that accompany this are exponential in their effect. While the multitude of competitive advantages taken for granted by Tier One and Tier Two companies are now gone, new, potentially ubiquitous advantages have arrived in the form of transformational technologies that are available to anyone able to access them through a connection to the web.

Of course the new GDE and marketplace are far more than e-commerce, which is simply a function and extension of the 'bricks and mortar' philosophy. e-Commerce is not an innovative and radical rethink, as it steps back from positing that the web will soon be, for all intent and purposes, the essential economy of the GDE and the 'real' world will simply exist to deliver what is agreed upon online. Coupled with the ever increasing acceptance of, and reliance upon, remote working and workers, this is proof – if it were needed – of the ever-increasing flattening of the world and the inherent me-conomics of the GDE. At an individual level, from mid-level employees to C-Level executives and above, the change is manifesting itself with a mighty wallop. The PHDs (Poor, Hungry and Driven) – as described by Matt Barrie in his interview (see page 22) – are chasing, and catching those, generally Western, MBAs (Marginalized By Audacity). The fact is, for years people have been taking their work home with them, and using their own devices to do so. Instead of resisting this process, it is incumbent upon mobile, agile organizations looking to thrive in the GDE/me-conomy, in the public or private sector, to embrace it.

It is true that existing approaches to corporate security do not always lend themselves to this embrace – yet. However, innovative technologies that are months, rather than years away, will enable the leveraging of legacy systems and existing capabilities, empowering said organizations, regardless of size, to surf the me-conomics of the GDE. There is a massive wave of opportunity coming, which can increase the stickiness, satisfaction and, most importantly, opportunity for all parties to profit.

What must also be acknowledged is that the number of people at this party is about to increase by orders of magnitude due to the advent of innovation in and around the use of mobile technology. There are over 6 billion mobile phone subscriptions worldwide; more than 5 billion of those are in the Majority World. These phones are currently being used as wallets, maps and tools to compare prices, etc. With the technology only now being released, they will, more and more, be used to recruit employees, do business, and collaborate on joint ventures. Smart phones and tablets will be the tools of choice to empower budding entrepreneurs around the world.

As the business world becomes flatter and horizons and time zones mean less and less, the Majority World is coming online and they are on point to take advantage of these tools' inherent agility and mobility. Traditional, massive multinational organizations have now got competition in the guise of new, mini-multinationals as companies on every continent embrace web-based technologies and social media, amongst other strategies. As such, they are becoming equally competitive on the commercial playing field of the GDE. Together, innovative technologies such as social media, Web 3.0 and the semantic web have changed the game. They will continue to do so, with ever increasing speed and power, in the competitive and cost-focused me-conomy of the GDE.

From here on in, businesses cannot believe that doing nothing is an option; it's not. Yes, we are in a time of flux, but that is precisely the time when businesses that seize upon the opportunities that innovation provides can come to the fore. Thinking you can sit back and watch this brass ring pass by is folly: if you don't grab it, someone else will. Organizations that don't increase their engagement with and empowerment of their endusers – who don't ensure that they are adaptable, agile and adept in the mobile arena – are likely to lose their slice of the GDE/me-conomy pie.

The following interviews are with business thought leaders and innovators from around the world. Each of them defines and delineates aspects of success and awareness of both the pitfalls and potentials inherent in this time of great opportunity.

Michael McDonald *Co-founder and CTO of KimmiC*

Since the late 1990s IT has been perceived as steadily failing to deliver simple business models and degenerating into a bureaucratic, inscrutable ivory tower when it comes to the strategic direction of the business. This, coupled with a changed world, in which billions are entering the new Global Digital Economy (GDE), means we have completely new business challenges and opportunities that aren't met by existing IT systems and approaches. The fact that Facebook and Twitter could hand the established players 'their lunch' shows how inadequate moving 1980s business concepts forward has been.

The problem has been: how to empower endusers in the new GDE? The lazy solution has often been the crux of the problem: the dreaded app. Why are apps the problem? Because they create and control their own abstract view on the world – this almost never is the same from app to app. The vendor has control over their abstract world and woe-betide any company that actually want access to, and control over, their underlying data.

Business units around the world are asking a simple question: 'The Cloud seems simple, I can access it on my phone or tablet – why can't IT be the same?' It's a brilliant question. Everything should be simple to access, 24/7, via mobile devices and individually customized for the enduser – not for marketers with a segmented push view on the world.

I created FlatWorld technology to answer the question: how can I (a person, business unit, company, etc) cooperate and share data simply (ie via a phone), securely (everything is encrypted, goodbye search engines, data miners, etc) with people, processes and the dreaded legacy applications. I want to do this in a mobile space, which is not only accessible 24/7 but is also simple to audit and, most importantly, where everyone can 'play well together', ie enabling moving/dynamic cooperation from all parties. This, combined with that ability to match any interaction to a business model of your making equates to the ability to create multitudes of high value, high touch markets; thus giving your company, or your data, a real shot at getting a hold in the new Global Digital Economy.

To build this and meet some pretty exacting criteria, especially from an existing 'Tier One' company perspective, was more than a challenge. This, combined with leveraging dual licence technologies means that the underlying economics of FlatWorld are cheaper than anyone – so it lives up to its name and ethos: creating a level playing field for any and all who want to engage in the GDE. Interesting times, yes – but doing nothing during this time of great change, is not an option.

INTERVIEWS

Julian Keith Loren

Julian is an award-winning innovator who has been building design and innovation teams and taking on large-scale, multi-faceted design challenges for over 20 years. Harnessing the power of gameplay to bridge disciplines and break communication barriers, Julian designs and facilitates Gameferences – unforgettable face-to-face games that drive deep exploration and breakaway design. He is the co-founder of the Innovation Management Institute where he has helped clients such as General Electric, Johnson & Johnson, eBay and the Institute for the Future with key innovation initiatives. Julian has also lectured and run collaborative design games at Stanford University and the University of California, Berkeley and occasionally writes about technology and innovation topics.

What are your thoughts about patent protection?

I was just consulting with a company that's one of the top five patent holders in the world. They have patents coming out of their ears, and most of the patents don't do anything for them anymore (besides creating additional expenses that they have to recoup).

They're desperate to do 'Super System Design' with unique business/ service models, organizational models, image models, and ecosystems and not try to protect themselves with patents anymore. That world is changing. Now, there are fewer spaces where patents still hold value, right? Software patents, specifically, often provide little or no protection.

How is this changing business models?

Patents keep certain managers and stockholders happy, but fewer and fewer. It used to be, if you were a start-up seeking funding, you had to get patents because the VC still cared. That game's changing.

Here in Silicon Valley, now it's: 'Show me a functioning business with people already in it. I'll invest in that. I don't care about your patent.' It's something that's been building for years, but had to reach this critical mass. Maybe, it hasn't [hit] everywhere, but definitely here in Silicon Valley, people are realizing it's not a patent game.

It sounds like the little guys who can be very agile around the feet of the, massive, monolithic companies may be well-placed to do well.

That depends. If you're a multi-million dollar company and you say, 'We're going to open up our innovation practice. We're going to create an open innovation network and we're looking for partners', you'll have a lot of small companies scrambling to be in that network. There are still competitive advantages related to scale, market penetration, brand recognition, etc. If you're starting your no-name company, how do you attract a large and vibrant ecosystem?

Big companies can take would-be competitors and make them product-enhancers... take all those 'little guy' start-ups and say, 'Actually, build on all the infrastructure we have; build on this wealth that we already have. You'll be more successful and you can focus on what differentiates you. We'll be your conduit to the market.' A lot of companies are seeing these opportunities and scrambling, to create these 'open innovation' networks of product- or service-enhancers.

> *Innovation has to be defined from the point of view of what it achieves, not from what it is. In this sense: Innovation = differentiation + $.*

Juan Cano-Arribí (Founder and CEO of Plantel)

You differentiate between innovators who are intrapreneurs and those who are entrepreneurs. How are they different?

I often describe myself as an intrapreneur. The intrapreneur has that same entrepreneurial spirit [as the entrepreneur] but also likes additional constraints, such as regulatory constraints or complex organizational dynamics to deal with. Either people hate that additional challenge or they love it. But, innovators, whether they're being entrepreneurs or intrapreneurs, are being change agents. Some people freely move back and forth and some people have a strong preference for one or the other.

I'm curious: who hires an intrapreneurial innovation consultant?

A lot of innovation consultants only do ideation and design facilitation, so it could be anyone in the organization who needs [those skills]. I try to steer clear of those ideation-only engagements. I come in on bigger projects and stay around for a longer part of the innovation cycle. They're often multi-billion dollar organizations with an audacious project – I don't take it unless it's audacious.

> *We're identifying what's happening on 'the edge' of business, which is largely driven by changes in digital platforms and helping businesses and organizations make sense of that. We advance the capability of organizations and individuals to make sense of the rapidly changing world and how to survive in it, as opposed to get smashed by it.*
>
> **Peter Williams** (Chief Edge Officer, Centre for the Edge Australia)

Keyword imagination exercise

Take a few minutes to close your eyes, relax and explore these keywords. You may want to make a note of any ideas that emerge that you want to explore later.

Audacious, Differentiate, Ecosystem, Infrastructure, Intrapreneur

Matt Barrie

A multi-award winning entrepreneur, technologist and lecturer, Matt Barrie is the founder and CEO of the world's largest outsourcing and crowdsourcing marketplace, Freelancer.com.

As an educator, an innovator and an entrepreneur, how do you define innovation?

The way I see it, it's looking at inefficient industries, processes and technologies – and the way they're doing things – and trying to come up with better solutions that make the world a better place, make life easier to live, and are better at making money.

Do you think that Australia is a good and supportive place to be an innovator?

Sure. Of the top 10 patent holders worldwide, I think we have the top five. In fact we've got the most prolific patent writer in the world, Kia Silverbrook, here.

It's a fantastic place to do research and development. There's a very great talent base to draw upon, there's good universities, and wells of research… And we certainly punch above our weight with a population of only 22 million people.

So, you don't feel 'Down Under' suffers under the tyranny of distance?

I think, in some ways, it's an advantage. Because we always think we're so far behind all the time, we're always trying to do better and better and, sometimes, we don't realize that we've actually surpassed the competition.

The good thing about the tyranny of distance is that we're always thinking about global markets. So a lot of people, from day one, are thinking, 'How do we crack the US market?' or, 'How do we get global from the start?'

For a lot of US companies that's a big failing they have. They'll say: 'Ok, we're in a great market, we can just focus on doing everything in America, in US dollars and the English language.' Companies will start up and do quite well in the US, but then get cloned and imitated around the world. Then they've got a real situation on their hands, which at some point they're going to have to try and mop up.

In the past, you have made it clear that you are less than impressed with the lack of emphasis Australian schools place on IT. Why is that?

The future of this country is not digging rocks out of the ground and shipping them overseas – we're running out of those minerals and natural resources. There're only one or two industries in the world where you can get tremendous productivity multipliers and contribute to wealth creation and really, it all comes down to technology.

We're 23 million people [in Australia] and the only way we're going to be able to play on the global scale, as a major player, is if we leverage the small talent base we have into something that's world scale. Technology is the place to do that. It should be a national imperative. We should have [the equivalent of] a space race, or Manhattan Project to try and build the technology industry in this country up to be world class.

At the moment we've got what our government calls the 'miracle economy'. It's only a miracle economy because the stuff that we dig out of the ground and ship overseas has been going up in price, thanks to China. That's the only reason we've got strong export growth. The windfall profits that we're making right now will become windfall losses as soon as the commodities cycle falls, and it look like it's doing that right now.

I believe the number one thing to do is to increase the level of education in the country, including in high schools. The big problem that Western nations have is the declining enrolment in engineering, computer science and the 'hard' sciences. This has been the case ever since the Moon landing. When we landed on the Moon every kid wanted to be an astronaut and they all enrolled in engineering courses. Since then enrolment [in the sciences] has been down year-on-year-on-year.

At the moment a lot of our tertiary educational institutions are only propped up because we bring fee-paying foreign students into the country to pay for the faculties. [We have] to encourage more high school students to get into technology and enrol in university. If we do that there will be more students to stay on to do advanced degrees, more research done, and more industries developed. There will be more people to start technology companies and go out there and solve the problems of the world and build wealth in the country. You can only get so far digging up dirt and shipping it overseas.

I think it's a national imperative and very inexpensive to do, in terms of helping build our education today. There's a complete revolution in the way education is being made available online now. We can deliver a very, very high quality programme, starting with teaching computer science to high school students, for only a couple of million dollars.

James Curran from the University of Sydney and Director of the National Computer Science School is prepared to develop this curriculum and deliver it. So it's a pretty simple choice for the [Australian] government, which is basically to say: 'Yes, let's do this.' Every kid has watched 'The Social Network'. Every kid wants to write an iPhone app or develop the next Facebook and surpass Mark Zuckerberg. We should allow them to do so. But, at the moment, we have a high school curriculum that is stagnant and stuck in the dark ages.

As a lecturer on technology venture creation do you see this topic as an inherent imperative?

The thing about technology is it's inherently entrepreneurial. If you look at the tech boom at the moment it's all about people starting companies and disrupting industries, and building big, long-term, sustainable, wealth-creating businesses.

When I went to university, in my under-grad, 20 years ago there was no exposure to the fact that you could be an entrepreneur or start your own company. The greatest exposure we had to that was, maybe, the examination of the product lifecycle of a business.

I'm running a programme, led by final-year engineers, where computer science students are given the exposure to, and confidence to use, frameworks and tools to enable them to think about starting businesses themselves.

If you look at what's happening worldwide, in the States and so forth, companies are coming out of nowhere and, in two and a half or three years, generating billions of dollars' worth of revenue in technology. There's a complete land grab on right now as the entire physical world transforms into a virtual economy – that's the internet.

The biggest direct marketing company is a software company: Google; the biggest book retailer – and soon to be the biggest retailer overall – in the world is a software company: Amazon; and the fastest growing telecoms company is a software company: Skype. This is the opportunity we need to capture, now, before someone else takes it away from us.

Looking at online business and the GDE, it's no surprise that I would look at your company, Freelancer, 'the world's largest outsourcing marketplace'. To my mind, Freelancer has increased the value of innovation because the people bidding on projects have to be innovative in order to win the job, whatever that job may be.

The great thing about Freelancer is that both sides of the marketplace are entrepreneurs. The entrepreneur in the West may be a small business owner or someone with an idea for a website or product or service. On the other side [of the equation], the freelancers are all entrepreneurs themselves. They're the elite of the elite of the elite of their economies. They may be in Bangladesh or India or Pakistan, or wherever, but they are the technological elite of their generation. They are going out there and starting companies. They're innovating and building things to help the rest of the world prosper. The great thing about the Freelancer marketplace is that everyone is there to innovate and be an entrepreneur.

> *Innovation is identifying unmet needs and developing solutions for them such that the market sucks them up.*
> **Larry MacDonald** (CEO and founder of Edison Innovations, Inc)

The innovation that is 'Freelancer' enables and empowers people from every corner of the world, as long as they have access to the internet. Obviously this includes people from the majority world who have, along with certain obstacles, the benefit of lower costs of living and of doing business. Do you think that their ability to charge less will have the overall effect of lowering the amount of money that can be made from doing a particular job?

The world is changing every day and technology is the major driver of this. I mean, we don't sell ice in the age of refrigerators. The world changes and jobs transform and the big challenge, for us in the West, is to move up the value chain and be the innovators and the entrepreneurs. We need to be the guys who ask: 'How do I create a job and not take a job?'

The fact of the matter is, there are 7 billion people on the planet and, at the moment, there are only 2 billion on the internet. But, there's another 5 billion soon to come. So, if you look at the global labour market, there is a huge amount of supply that's about to come online.

We can put our head in the sand and wish that it wasn't going to happen, but the fact of the matter is there are 5 billion people that are poor, hungry and driven – I call them PHDs – who are connecting to the internet now, and want a job. They're surviving today on $8 a day or less, sometimes $2 a day or less, and sometimes less than that. [Freelancer is a] great opportunity for these entrepreneurs, in those developing countries, to go online and earn their monthly salaries, literally in hours or days.

Yes, there are risks for the West. But the risks are not going to be in the jobs that have entrepreneurial flair, critical reasoning, or big technical specialist skills. And they're not going to be in the blue-collar jobs: the plumbers, the tradesmen, the people who park the cars, and what have you. But if you're stuck in the middle, in a white-collar job where your job can effectively be described by an algorithm – or, as Tom Friedman said, if your job can be better done by a piece of software or a website…

There are lots of these jobs around. I'll walk into a bank, a rental car company, a real estate office or an accounting firm – even, in some regards, some forms of law practice – there's a lot of people doing work that's really inefficient and can be better done by a piece of software or, maybe, by someone else.

The challenge for us here in the West is to move up the value chain. We [need to] increase the education of our workforce, and our population, and do things like teach high school students about technology properly, not just give lip service to it. We need to put the proper effort into turning our universities into world-class educational institutions at the cutting edge of research and science.

> How many of our entrepreneurs are solving India's problems? We must not get enamoured by the tremendously successful models of the West and turn a blind eye to the severely localized challenges that are unique only to India. Within India, many other micro-countries exist. With such a large consumer base, entrepreneurs and start-ups can intelligently target the right market to go after and still build a sizable business if they are not addressing the entire country. The quality of entrepreneur in India is getting better and better. Our new generation of entrepreneurs have an enviable blend of high IQ, humility, global exposure and access to the best tech talent in the world. The possibilities of building extremely competitive global businesses from India are limitless. There's no reason the next Facebook, Dropbox or Airbnb can't be built in India.

Kunal Shah (Founder and CEO of FreeCharge.in)

Keyword imagination exercise

Change, Competition, Disruptive, Entrepreneur, Risk

Tara Hunt

Speaker, author and award-winning entrepreneur and influencer, Tara Hunt is founder and CEO of the innovative online retail site, Buyosphere.

Photo Credit: Lane Hartwell

You have worn many hats in your career, for instance alongside #pinko marketing, you were also heavily involved in the early co-working movement. How did you find yourself there?

At the time that I was starting with co-working I was working at a dot com start-up, but I was already thinking about becoming more independent – a freelancer working with various projects and with other start-ups. Selfishly I also kind of needed a space to reach out. So, it all started coming together, and I was surrounding myself with the right people.

My business partner, and boyfriend at the time, was really passionate about these things as well. We spent a lot of time talking about how democratized conferences and spaces could change the world, and it really has evolved to do that. Co-working has evolved into some pretty amazing spaces, in multiple cities, around the world. A lot of organizations have opened their desks because they see the innovative ability of having strangers come into your office; it works better.

Do you see it as somehow helping to foster innovation in business or in how business is done?

In our wildest dreams we didn't imagine that it would actually start to involve really big organizations, and that they would become more innovative by doing this internally and inviting external people to participate. That's a really cool evolution.

How did you come to understand that 'eating your own dog food' is an imperative?

If I'm not using my own product I'm not finding ways in which others may be becoming frustrated with it, not telling us, and just leaving. It's the best way to figure out what the points of frustration are for your user base or the reason why your user base isn't growing.

 Do the work.

Scott Heiferman (Co-founder and CEO of Meetup)

There is a small, wonderful number of people that will actually stop and write you an e-mail, send you a tweet or post on your wall, saying that they're having a problem. And those wonderful people I keep very close to me; but there's a much larger group of people that will try out your site, have a bad experience, shrug their shoulders and move on to the next thing. At every point I've figured out what is wrong with the experience, where we're not nailing the issue or solving the problem. By doing it I'm interacting with the user base that is there and figuring out what everybody else is responding to as well.

Would you say that Buyosphere is a reflection of, or maybe a growth from, the #pinko consumer-to-consumer marketing you pioneered?

Yes, absolutely. It really is about putting the customer at the centre of everything. The whole idea behind #pinko marketing was: the 'pinkos' were communist sympathizers and #pinko marketing is about customer sympathizers – a marketer who thinks like a customer, and puts the customer at the centre.

[Initially] it was a scary concept for a lot of brands because they were used to command and control – controlling the brand image and voice – but it has become a huge reality: the biggest, loudest voices for any brand are the customers. That's how Buyosphere works – pure recommendation.

It's the pull instead of the push. And it could be said that #pinko is part of the consumer revolution; and if organizations and companies don't cater to the revolutionaries – their empowered consumers/end users – well, they may not lose their head, but they will certainly lose their slice of the marketplace pie.

Absolutely. I would say that the revolution is here and it's definitely affecting sales, but the retailers haven't gotten on board yet.

And look at what's happening to retail as an industry – it's haemorrhaging cash. What are your thoughts on how innovation in e-commerce will continue to change the retail industry? For instance is it removing the great need for brick and mortar businesses and storefronts by replacing them with virtual malls?

I can see the virtual shopping malls for sure, but there's actually an interesting phenomenon happening. A lot of e-commerce sites are starting to open flagship stores, because they're realizing the importance of trying things on, touching fabrics, and feeling comfortable with the brand.

I think there is always going to be a space for a physical, brick and mortar space, but they're going to change quite a bit. There's going to be a more fluid interaction between online and offline stores. A few big retailers in the US are allowing customers to order online and pick up in-store; and when you order in online, and if you don't like something or it doesn't fit you, you can exchange it in the store.

How do you see e-commerce being able to harness the economy of attention?

I'm going to sound a little bit socialist for American taste but it can put us in a position where people – customers – have enough tools available to them that we all buy better. We don't buy more – we buy better. I guess that's more hopeful on my part than necessarily fortune telling, but you've got to create a world that you want to live in.

I'm aware that you were living in America as an immigrant and brought a great deal to that nation. Would it be fair to say that many Americans aren't aware of how incredibly important innovative immigrants are to their nation as a whole and certainly to their economic base?

Well, first of all they don't call us immigrants – they call us aliens which, I think, defines the sentiment about who we are as residents of the US. They see us as taking jobs and opportunities away from Americans... even if Google was founded by two immigrants at the end of the day.

> *Innovation has grown leaps and bounds from the turn of the century and now into the new millennial age. Innovation is no longer coming up with a simple invention: innovation is the gathering of resources and talent, creating a platform, harnessing that platform and affecting change. Moving forward, I believe that the innovations being made today will allow for the continued and rapid repair to the past generation's idea of innovation.*
>
> **Khayyam Wakil** (Chief Innovation Officer at Immersive Media)

Keyword imagination exercise

Consumer, Empower, Interaction, Revolution, User

Vincent Carbone

Vincent Carbone is co-founder and COO of Brightidea. Over the past decade he has specialized in the implementation of strategic innovation programmes and is working towards building a global innovation grid.

Did you name your company Brightidea as homage to Thomas Edison? I ask, as I note that you were born in Edison and grew up in Menlo Park, New Jersey.

Menlo Park was the first place that had electric street lights because Thomas Edison's lab was around the corner. Frankly, Edison was the godfather of idea management. We trace our roots back to him as what we're doing at Brightidea is helping companies manage innovation. He was one of the first people to document and track ideas – all of his ideas – on filed index cards so he could go back, cross-reference and build upon them.

And as such, respect for the idea is absolutely apparent in his professionalism.

I've never heard anybody say, 'respect for the idea', but I think that nails it. He had respect for every idea. And that's something that people and companies need to start doing: respecting all ideas as having some intrinsic value to them, and putting in some kind of infrastructure to track, record and capture that intrinsic value.

I think that companies are just starting to realize there is intrinsic value in each idea; the reason: because the world is becoming digitalized. As the world becomes digitalized, it becomes easier and easier to make things. The 3D printer is the embodiment of being able to make anything that you can think of.

As things become more digitalized and it gets easier and easier to manufacture goods, the intrinsic value of raw ideas, early ideas, all ideas actually increases because the barrier to the creation of those things is getting lower and lower. You know the saying, '1 percent inspiration, 99 percent perspiration'? I think, because of the world getting digitalized that equation is starting to shift and become more balanced.

On the Brightidea website you state that, once created, the innovation grid will be 'an intricate web of interlocking ideas', which 'may hold the potential to solve our world's greatest challenges'. Do you see those ideas as potentially being commodities in and of themselves, which can be sold and traded; and, therefore, would your innovation grid be some kind of innovation or idea stock market?

That's exactly right. That's what we're hinting at. Let's say General Electric and Lockheed, and their employees, come up with ideas for things that may not be directly related to their particular companies. What if, for instance, there were incentive schemes for employees to contribute ideas and for companies to realize the intrinsic value in those ideas? Over time we'll see companies moving into the business of ideas. Some ideas are going to drive their own products and services. But for other ideas the most effective return on the investment might be to sell them to someone else that can leverage them.

Once the innovation grid gets to a critical mass, those opportunities will present themselves and, hopefully, we will be able to be the eBay of that exchange. We really do believe that this can help human beings, help the world and better our planet in the long run.

Creativity and understanding are the cornerstones. When the understanding is insulated from the change occurring outside the company, it is inwardly biased. Having worked with foresight, as a key tool for decision making, and the rapidly changing technology opportunities, I think it is paramount to add 'outnovation'; to focus equally on the different: business models, industries, human behaviours, technologies and competitors.

This happens most naturally when leaders have understood that creativity is at the heart of good leadership, not rote decisions. The best outcomes happen when curiosity and creativity meet business agency; a resilience and ability to make things happen, taking into consideration the context of now and hope for and understanding of the future. A critical aspect of this is that one individual cannot cover the demands of thought and action alone. To enact the thought, the people involved need to understand, as relevant in their roles, the bigger picture. Hence the good way to do this is always with a cascade of understanding and collaboration. This can be done in a minimal way or when need be as a major programme but the fundamental remains: the best way to activate a future is to co-create it.

Dominique Jaurola (Mobile/internet entrepreneur – futurist)

Keyword imagination exercise

Collaborate, Digital, Tool, Value, World

Matt Flannery

Matt Flannery is the CEO and co-founder of Kiva, which uses innovation in technology and micro finance to work towards the alleviation of poverty. He is a recipient of *The Economist's* No Boundaries Innovation Award.

On the face of it, when you decided to ask strangers to lend money to other strangers in a bid to use micro-finance to alleviate poverty and empower individuals in the Majority World... well, I imagine some people might have thought you were crazy to try and do something like Kiva?

People said it wouldn't scale; people in Africa couldn't get all their data onto the internet; we couldn't get the money to them; no one would pay back their loans. They said it was illegal, infeasible, not possible and so on. Yeah, in general, that it wouldn't work.

One thing that helped it work was assembling a group of people that, though they didn't know if it was going to work, worked as a great team. When you're working on something that might not work, it requires a lot of trust and intimacy; the people involved have to agree to do something together – something that people on the outside are saying won't work. It requires a lot of trust.

What was your driver for beginning the Kiva initiative?

In 2004, when I was 27 years old, I went on a trip to Uganda, Kenya and Tanzania with my co-founders Jessica and Moses. I was just doing it as a break from my work as a computer programmer at TiVo. I was volunteering with a non-profit, interviewing people who were taking small business loans to do things like start a fish-selling business, a seamstress business, a clothes reselling business or a small restaurant. I was really inspired by their stories.

I was making a video, interviewing these people, and I thought it was really inspiring. I had an image of Africa that was based on starvation, warfare, disease and other depressing things, and what I found was a lot of uplifting stories and entrepreneurs that, quite frankly, I really related to.

I'm somebody that likes entrepreneurship; I was always trying to start businesses myself. So, rather than emphasizing people's suffering, I found myself enjoying talking to people about their strategies and their plans for the future. It was a really uplifting, hopeful time.

I loved it and wanted to share it with my friends, so we created the Kiva website to give Americans the experience that we had in Africa: learning about business ideas and joining in partnership with business people, rather than taking pity on them. It's about fostering relationships based on partnership and mutual dignity rather than a patronage or a benefactor relationship.

In the end, innovation only succeeds when it's a clear expression of the brand, which is to say that the product – whatever it is – has to be compelling, differentiated and true. Something that's compelling motivates people to action: that's the point, even if 'action' refers to a state of mind. A product that is well-differentiated isn't just unique, but makes it obvious why your offering is preferable to any of your competitors. Most importantly, innovation has to be true: True as in no-hyperbole; true as in an unshakable commitment to authenticity, to keeping promises, and to quality; true as in connected to purpose, to customer, and to the communities you serve. Sure, innovation that's novel gets noticed, but innovation that's compelling, differentiated and true is what gets adopted.

Cecily Sommers (Author and strategy and innovation consultant)

And you're looking to build more relationships with your latest endeavour, Kiva Zip. What effect do you look for from that project?

Zip.kiva.org is an experiment we're running; we don't know exactly where it's going to go but it has a lot of potential. Kiva's mission is to connect people, through lending, to alleviate poverty. We're trying to do both those things, with this project, to a greater degree. It represents an attempt to both increase the level of connection between people and to reach people that are left out of the world's financial system.

In Kenya, which is particularly innovative, we're connecting lenders and borrowers directly through their mobile phones – borrowers post their phone number and a picture and we lend to them directly over the internet. Some of these people live outside of Kenyan towns or on islands off the coast. These people are pretty far out: they're people in slums, getting loans of $60 or less, that are left out of both the banking, and non-profit banking, sector in Kenya. We're able to reach them directly, at a cheaper price, by sending small 0 percent interest loans directly to their phones.

When we started doing this there were so many people that thought it wasn't going to work. First of all, the technology is just coming around to making it possible. There're a lot of questions and unknowns, but it's going pretty well. It's not perfect, but we're learning every day. Our repayment rate is around 97 percent – not 99 percent, like it is on Kiva.org – but it's higher than the US credit card repayment rate, [which] hovers at around a 60 percent on-time repayment rate.

What we're noticing is we're increasing empathy with both the lenders and the borrowers that we work with, so Kiva is a vessel for increasing empathy and compassion around the world. Imagine classrooms of kids that grew up lending on Kiva and had an early experience of a connection with somebody in Israel, Palestine or South Sudan, for instance. Imagine how that will affect them when they become adults and they're making choices about their career, or when they're in politics and have to make important decisions. They will be part of a generation with more empathy because of the connected web and things like Kiva. It will be harder to have a sense of someone as an enemy when you grew up connected to them.

Kiva connections and initiatives are certainly illustrating the power of enduser enablement.

We're just one organization serving a cause that's much bigger than our organization, but we can play a big role. What we're noticing is we're increasing empathy with both the lenders and the borrowers that we work with.

We had a guy from Mexico come and talk about his work with bio-digesters in Mexico that were getting Kiva loans, from a hundred or more people on Kiva. He spoke about the effect the loans had on the psychology of the recipients. These are pretty poor people that haven't travelled and that no one was paying attention to. Now they can see the faces of the hundred-plus people supporting them. They know that someone – be it in Hong Kong, Sweden or Seattle – took the time to lend $25, write a comment, and is genuinely interested in their business, which involves decomposing cow manure and turning it into gasoline in rural Mexico.

That can have a transformative effect on somebody, once they realize that they are a global citizen and a part of something bigger. These people know that if they repay their loan, that will enable someone else like them, whether they're in Mexico or Africa, to get a loan. They realize their micro-actions have bigger implications somewhere halfway across the world.

I used to think of innovation in terms of coming up with a new way to solve a problem – pretty typical definition. But over the last 10 years or so I've come to see innovation as being much less connected to the idea itself, and much more about mental, physical, and financial fortitude, ie can you take your idea and realize it? Chances are that 50 people will have your idea at exactly the same time, but it's a 'tree falling in a forest with no one around' scenario. For the innovation to actually occur in a way that matters, someone has got to spend their life savings (or social capital) pulling the tree out of the forest, standing it up again, gathering a crowd around, and then tipping it over again and again and again, until the crowd actually gives a damn about this tree... which is extremely unlikely in the first place. So, if you can do better than Sisyphus at this game, well then you've really innovated. Kudos if you can actually love the exercise of it; and extra kudos if you can make some money doing it.

Ben Rigby (CEO of Sparked.com)

Keyword imagination exercise

Connect, Empathy, Inspire, Majority, Trust, World

Yobie Benjamin

Entrepreneur, technology innovator and inventor, Yobie Benjamin is the CTO for Citigroup and Chairman of Citigroup's GTS Development Innovation and Learning Centres. He has also been named as one of the top security professionals in the world by 20/20 and the Discovery Channel.

How do you see digital finance fitting in to the economy?

When you say 'digital', I say that's clearly part of the mobile agenda. I have this theory: generally, everybody on the planet has, what I call, a personal economic ecosystem. In the West [these ecosystems] are really large, in breadth and depth.

You have a car, so you can move from one location to another and commerce will occur; mobility has a profound effect. Communications is another thing that has a profound effect on a very wide and very deep personal economic ecosystem. Your ability to talk to people, to communicate via the internet to others, really expands that [ecosystem]. In fact, most people in the West can do anything because of communication, telecommunications, and transportation. But, that's only about 20–25 percent of the planet.

We now go to what we derisively know as the 'emerging world' – the rest of the people on the planet. They do not have cars, therefore they have no mobility; and they are just discovering the notion of a mobile phone.

The mobile phone has largely played two roles. Its first role is voice communications; so, suddenly, they can talk to their cousin in the next village. It's also given rise to a certain level of functional literacy: they can text message now. That very basic functional literacy has a profound effect on the way they can expand their personal economic ecosystem.

They're now not only communicating by voice: they're actually communicating digitally in a way that uses some notion of a written language, whatever the written language may be. This has expanded access exponentially... it's been a quantum leap in access.

Suddenly, the person in Bamako, Mali, has the ability to sell something to somebody in Sierra Leone or in Guinea; that's a huge deal! They never had that before. Their notion of trading, of commerce, has always been a function of proximity, of location: the ability to travel, whether by horse, donkey, or some notion of public transport. They knew a very limited notion of commerce and payments.

Suddenly this economic ecosystem, which was almost solely the purview and privilege of the West, is beginning to go into the rest of the world, the world that has the biggest population [the Majority World]. The world that by sheer population growth, will have a more profound impact than all the Western world and, by the way, will achieve far higher levels of productivity because of this digital enablement.

When you look at the Global Digital Economy, how would you compare the need for innovation in Tier One companies to the need for innovation in what I call 'Tier None' companies?

Generally, the larger the company, the less innovative it is, and not because it doesn't want to be: it's an organizational issue. Any large organism is, by nature, very complex. A single human cell is very simple. But, when you expand it to look at the entire human body, it's very complicated. When you look at nations, a single citizen is not very complicated, but if it becomes a village, a state and a nation, it becomes very complex.

The issues of governance, control, rules and regulations, and social justice all become exceedingly complicated as organizations become larger. So, by definition, smaller organizations are probably going to be the fountainhead of innovation. They can move faster, quicker and cheaper.

So would you say that 'innovation has a nation'?

I don't think it is the purview only of those people in more advanced nations or those who have advanced educational degrees. For instance, I have a Bachelor of Arts in Broadcast Communications and I am self-taught in computer science... and guess what? I am the Global Chief Technology Officer of a very large bank.

You give those of us with a liberal arts education great hope! Speaking of hope, your 'hobby' of working in the field of genetic modification is one that could bring great hope to a vast number of people.

Right now, as a hobby, we're designing viruses and bacteria to kill cancer cells. It's an emerging area of biology called 'synthetic biology'. Synthetic biology is the science, and the art, of taking the most fundamental computer and trying to program it. And what is the most fundamental computer? It's human life. Cells and viruses are, fundamentally, computers that you can program. They have an input and output... a bacterium is the same. So the question is: now that we know how they behave and what inputs and outputs are expected, how can we manipulate DNA in order for such things to become tools for good – for, let's say, curing cancer?

Yeast, interestingly enough, is very close to the human DNA structure; and we can manipulate yeast. Brewer's yeast happens to be the foundation for all bread and for beer. To be able to prove that you can manipulate a simple organism, such as yeast, and put in some cancer-fighting base pairs, is a pretty powerful concept.... We could say, 'Drink this beer, it's genetically modified to cure your cancer.' It could be done; we know we have the science to do it.

Yet, you are living in a nation – the United States – where you are going to come up against some people who may not support your work and, in fact, may attempt to legislate against it.

That's absolutely correct. It is likely a political question; but those political barriers and walls vary from country to country. And guess what? I'm an American, but I'm also a global citizen. Meaning that, if I can't do it here, there are nearly 200 countries in the world and I can choose where I do it.

At some point the reality of the global village is going to dawn on people. They're going to say: 'Fine. If you don't want me to do it here then I will do it elsewhere.' I can do it in Sweden, in Australia or an island nation like Nauru – a country that is slowly digging out all its phosphates to the point of the annihilation of the entire country.

If the world had iron fences and was somewhat monolithic then yes, that would be a problem. But the world is not monolithic, politics are not monolithic. There are governments and nations and states that are more willing to [make] advances in health science over what I consider irrational fears.

Disruption is the necessary element in order to innovate and innovation is hugely global. In ProVoke I have a theory called the 'three-legged stool', which says that in order for us to make progress, we have to think about disruption and progress is like a stool that has three legs.

The first leg is top-down. It's imperative that the management, executives and board of a company believe innovation is important and support it. Not just saying, 'We should innovate', but really support it and put together metrics for rewarding individual [employees, rather than] reprimanding them for lack of focus because they spent time on innovating.

The second leg of the stool is the bottom-up, which is the rank and file in the company – particularly a very successful, large company. These individuals have to start taking risks and believing that innovation can happen.

And thirdly, there's the centre-forward, which is the organization as a whole embracing the concept of innovation, some level of risk-taking, and the likelihood of some level of failure (which they will reward, not reprimand, people for).

We need to focus on this three-legged concept, because if any one of the legs is missing the stool tilts over. We need to learn to embrace risk, failure and fear in order to become passionate and achieve huge innovation success.

Linda Bernardi (Author and innovation consultant)

Keyword imagination exercise

Communication, Fear, Global, Mobile, Platform

Final thoughts

It's undeniable: the world's economy is changing and it may be a bumpy ride – more so for some than others. The new, knowledge-based GDE (the e-conomy of e-commerce) can be equated to something like the Wild West of yore, in its current state of flux and free-for-all for online stakes. But, unlike the classic Western, the heroes of this economic era will not be those who stand still, silent and alone. The success stories of the GDE will be those businesses and organizations that collaborate and communicate with each other and with their ever-more expectant, empowered endusers – those who put the 'me' in the me-conomy. Together, they face a frontier which, though admittedly often uncertain, is borderless and boundless in its potential.

The state of the nation addressed

Taking stock of how things stack up

02

Accountable, Affordable, Barrier, Broadband, Constraints, Data, Distribution, Diversity, Embrace, Empathize, Future, GDE, GDP, Identity, Impact, Involved, Knowledge, Mission, Network, Opportunity, Participation, Plan, Problem, Responsibility, Solution, Talent, Transparency, Values, Vision, Women

Every year the President of the United States reports on the condition of the country and his plans for moving it forward, via his State of the Union Address. I believe that it is incumbent upon all of us, wherever we may live, to address the state of our own particular nation's innovation. We must look at it from a micro, macro and supra-national perspective because innovation – in all its guises – has a profound effect on us all – personally and professionally – as individuals, communities, nations and global citizens. (And, quite frankly, we undoubtedly have an effect on it, and its propensity for success on the local and global stage.)

Even if you don't have a passport – and let's face it, the majority of the world's population does not – you are a citizen of the world. As such, the effect that innovation has on you – particularly economically and, more and more, politically – will only continue to grow. That said, I wonder: does innovation have a 'nation'; does it have a home where it is more valued, more acknowledged for being an imperative to moving society forward? Though there are those who, optimistically – and debatably – would opine that innovation has the potential to bring out the best in people, what is without doubt is that the prosperity of a nation and the communities within it will become ever-more reliant on innovation and its easy accessibility.

Communities throughout the world, be they villages, towns, cities, states or nations, will both consciously and unconsciously, have an ever increasing appetite for innovation. This may manifest itself in a myriad of ways. It may be in an unceasing thirst for ever faster, ever quicker internet connectivity – broadband or otherwise. Perhaps it will be illustrated by a resolution to reduce reliance on carbon-based fuels and their current, gargantuan footprint on a fragile ecosystem. Already there is the determination to create new economies that empower local control and diversity, as they engage in the flattening world of the Global Digital Economy (GDE). It is certainly conspicuous in the increasing awareness of engaged citizens/endusers that, via systems such as social media and online participatory politics, there can be a transparency of and control over legislative issues as never before.

As these issues, and many more, are made apparent, it will be through innovation, innovative thought and innovative leadership, that their solutions are designed and brought to pass. It will become more evident that it is nations with a vision that involves the inherent innovative capability of a workforce that is multicultural, multi-ethnic and immigration-friendly, which will be more likely to thrive rather than just survive in the new, knowledge-based GDE. They will be nations comprised of smart, innovative communities, companies and businesses.

Regardless of their size, smart, collaborative communities are the engines that will drive the GDE. For these communities to flourish, an underlying innovative spirit and infrastructure are necessary. This infrastructure includes accessible, affordable, services such as healthcare, education and transportation, as well as a leadership that acknowledges the inherent importance of innovation and innovative approaches to longstanding problems. Initial steps towards this may be evidenced by the appointment of national chief innovation officers and ministers for innovation, such as Fleur Pellerin of France, Australia's Greg Combet, Genc Pollo of Albania, Vince Cable in the UK and the United States' Steven VanRoekel; as well as at the municipal level by San Francisco's CIO Jay Nath and Rahul Merchant in New York, to name but a few.

Now is the time when the need for innovation and innovative leadership is imperative. Let me state it plainly: we are approaching a tipping point where nations that do not innovate will be left behind to meander through the mire of an economic morass from which they may not recover. Businesses small and large, organizations both public and private, and governments around the world must focus their efforts on thriving in the new GDE.

As oil wells run dry and industries evolve to rely less on ores dug out of large holes in the ground, nations with economies that currently rely on natural resources may find themselves holding onto a shovel that delivers decidedly less booty into their coffers. Natural resources may be a short-term blessing but a long-term curse to a nation looking to succeed in the competition for innovation. By overemphasizing the importance of mining, for instance, and undervaluing the importance of a technologically collaborative ecosystem of innovation, many nations will suffer a 'brain drain' as more and more innovators – particularly those with an entrepreneurial spirit – head offshore to develop and capitalize on their ideas. It is the nations with a vision and plan that will prosper and, through the exploitation of the intelligence of their population and the support of the entrepreneurial spirit therein, have the greatest opportunity to thrive in the new GDE.

It is incumbent upon governments, at all levels, to put strategic and structural plans into place that leverage the InQ – the Innovation Quotient – of their workforce and education system. Additionally, there must be a strong, user-friendly infrastructure to support collaborative cooperative innovation. This includes but certainly isn't limited to mobile phone penetration, internet pervasiveness and easily affordable mobile data.

Every year the World Economic Forum publishes a Global Competitiveness Report that ranks nations on factors such as goods and labour market efficiency, business sophistication, and technological readiness and innovation, which has become a major determining factor in the standings. In the 2012–13 report, in second spot, Singapore was the only non-European nation in the top five. Topped by Switzerland, the other nations rounding out the first five are Finland, Sweden and the Netherlands. What are some of the traits shared by these countries? All have ministries focused on innovation and all share an awareness of the importance of linking innovation with education, business and infrastructure so as to benefit their nation's economies and their citizen's potential to thrive in the new GDE.

Certain nations are – I believe to their detriment in the innovation stakes – renowned for the risk aversion of their populations. Though it is, admittedly, difficult to legislate, governments that encourage their citizens to take calculated risks are more likely to have innovations to hand upon which economies can flourish. Innovators constantly face the likelihood of failure. The fact that they move forward in the face of this Sisyphean situation, which sees them repeatedly guiding their innovations up the steep hill of potential while aware that they could just as easily roll back and crush them, is what separates them from the 'would haves' and 'could haves'. The last thing they need is a government that ignores their achievements, let alone lies in wait to punish them for any failures they may meet along the way with such things as credit blacklisting, perennial personal liability and equating failure with fraud.

Additionally, the innovation-stifling 'tall poppy' syndrome, where individuals who strive to 'put their head above the parapet' or 'stand out from the crowd' are frowned upon, can be extremely deleterious to an innovative society. Perhaps a belief that 'anything is possible' is as relevant and useful as 'out of the box' thinking and resolute resourcefulness to an aspiring innovative society and the communities celebrating the problem-solving capacity of the innovative individuals within them.

It is valid to question whether innovation is political. I do not think it is, in and of itself. However, I wonder whether the support for innovation, or its lack, is differentiated by partisan politics. Does it matter where you're located in the world for the importance of innovation to be made manifest and for its success to be acknowledged and openly applauded? Is innovation stymied in societies that are less democratic, or where capitalism is free to run roughshod over regulation? Can one have capitalistic free rein in cultures that are politically communal or socially-democratic, rather than fully committed to a free market? Should governmental policy be imposed to support innovation in society? Are countries that have a population struggling to feed themselves more likely to be innovative out of necessity? Is there a difference between innovation to survive and innovation to thrive?

There is likely to be no definitively right or wrong answer to these questions. However, what is certain is that citizens in all of those societies, through the advent of and access to innovative technology are becoming more empowered and engaged. The coming era is that of the empowered citizen/enduser – those who were, until recently, often ignored. They are becoming stronger, louder and more emboldened. This is a good thing, as it is a sign of a healthy, innovative society – one that is not frightened of non-conformist, creative thinkers within its midst.

Empowered citizens are discovering their ability to influence political parties and policy through muscular use of social media: they are Society 2.0. This marries well with the advent of OpenGov (Open Government) and the application of increased government transparency, where anyone can access public data in new, beneficial ways through the use of innovative technology and tools – aka Gov 2.0 and e-Gov. This e-Gov interaction of participatory politics is a transformational, two-way street. Just as citizens are capable of connecting with Gov 2.0, innovation-minded governments have the capability to connect with their citizens – to learn from them and better service their clearly defined and refined wants and needs. Around the world, cities such as San Francisco and Seoul have a vision, mission and plan for e-Gov success, with initiatives such as implementing the use of mobile devices to improve the delivery of public services.

It is unlikely that innovation is specific to any particular country, culture or citizenry. But, I believe, the state of a nation's innovation can be judged by its government's commitment to the social welfare of its people, the empowerment engendered by its provisioning of a decent education to everyone, the accessibility of a collaborative, cooperative technological infrastructure, and its acknowledgement that the failure of an idea does not equate to the failure of the innovative ideal.

David Ben-Kay

Founder and Chairman of the Yuanfen-Flow Consulting Studio

Innovation is collaborative, cross-disciplinary solutions that address problems facing the planet and mankind.

INTERVIEWS

Richard Boly

Richard Boly is Director of the Office of e-Diplomacy at the US Department of State. He is a leader in transnational entrepreneurial ecosystems such as Mind the Bridge and a highly regarded supporter of international innovation and innovators.

Photo credit: Teck Kong Lee

Diplomacy in itself is something of a juggling routine, and to have added an 'e' to the remit must require an extremely deep and wide range of experiences and expertise. I'd think being somewhat light on your feet, as it were, would also be quite useful.

Innovators embrace constraints. So if you are a start-up company in Silicon Valley, your constraints are: the amount of money that you've been able to raise; the quality of talent that you've been able to put together; and your ability to hit the marketplace ahead of your competitors with a solution. In that environment you may wish that you had more money, had another coder, and/or had more time to get to the window. You have to embrace the constraints that you face or you're really on a fool's errand.

Likewise, people working in government need to [do the same]. If you want to innovate here, you need to embrace the constraints of a shorter budget or a longer decision process. You innovate within the constraints that you find yourself in.

So you can use, if not innovation, then innovative thought as an aid in diplomacy both within the State Department and in dealings with other US agencies and other nations?

Definitely. I think the trick is your balance. I think of a silly analogy but: if you are riding a wind sailboard you could turn really quickly because you don't have much gravity. You don't have much to weight to you so the impact that you have is relatively small. You're very agile.

If you're sitting on top of a battleship, that same sail that you could turn nimbly with on the sailboard wouldn't make an impact on the trajectory of the battleship. But, it's got a huge potential impact. It's gathered a lot of weight and gravity, so while it's not immediately perceptible, the ability to make that small change – that one-tenth of one degree of change – over the course of months and years, becomes significant.

And, it's being able to change your horizon and understand the impact of decisions today, six months, a year, five years from now. While you may not be around to reap the benefits, and nobody may remember that you were the person or your team was the one to start that turn or that tack, the satisfaction is in doing the right thing and in being the change agent at the moment.

It's often better to ask someone to turn one degree and see how far they can travel than to try to get them make a 180 degree flip. I would think that's quite relevant when it comes to diplomacy and politics.

Yes. Governments, in general, are 'risk-givers' and diplomacy, even among government cohorts, are 'risk-givers'. It's by design. You don't want your diplomats out there winging it if they're negotiating some important agreement with a foreign government.

How does your passion for entrepreneurship and innovative ideas, along with your interest in social justice – exemplified by your work with the Mind the Bridge Foundation, the United Way and the Peace Corp – inform your work at the State Department?

I'm a big believer in strongly advocating through your position [until a] decision's made. Then, if you're on the losing side, it's important not to try to undercut the decision that's been made. Which, in part, is why I often look to do work in green-field areas where no decision has been made yet, or where you're ahead of the decision.

For instance, in Paraguay I was working with the judiciary. [I said] look, your judges and your prosecutors are trained in how to enforce intellectual property rights laws, which are strong and clearly defined in Paraguay. You've got third parties who are helping to identify the people breaking the law, so you've got added resources to support your prosecutors. And the 'bad' people are people who [get] money by funnelling knockoff products [and they] fund terrorism and drug dealers. This all reflects poorly on Paraguay. Let's take this perfect storm of opportunity and help turn a corner for Paraguay so that it's a place where [people] can do business.

As you've mentioned intellectual property (IP): what are your thoughts about the argument for the elimination of patents, due to their supposed ineffectiveness? Some argue that patents are akin to trade barriers, and may even slow economic growth.

I know that there are a lot of nuances that go on in what's considered intellectual property... and the paradigm is going to evolve, especially with these erratically evolving digital components. But, just look at the growth in many societies of an innovative class; largely it has been accompanied by the 'creative' class [and their] ability to have their innovations protected.

The example I use is from my time in Italy. We used to talk to the Italian government and say, 'Of course [we] care about intellectual property protections to ensure that US companies are paid fairly for whatever property they've produced. But you, Italy, should care about it because your indigenous Italian innovators have gone on to create billions of dollars of market capital and create tens of thousands of jobs with their innovations, they just haven't done it in Italy.'

They've gone to Switzerland, the UK or the United States, to start companies like Logitech. In part, because they were concerned that their intellectual property won't be protected here. It's in the interest of countries that want to have high paying, high skilled knowledge worker jobs, to create an environment where people will innovate in the space [and] not go somewhere else, where they think they're going to be better protected.

There is the open source community; it's a powerful and very important part of the creative software marketplace. But there are also people saying: 'Look, investors are investing in us because we're going to build something that will create value to society and people are willing to pay for that value. We get something out of that, our investors get something out of that, and hopefully society's better off because of the product that we produced – that is a net plus.'

With that in mind and in particular noting your work with the global entrepreneurship programme, do you think that innovation has a nation?

I think that location and ecosystems matter; they matter a lot. What we found in Italy, just as an example, [was] there's great research but very little connection between research and the marketplace. And identifying and promoting entrepreneurial role models is extremely important.

This may be a silly analogy, but: if you go to a beautiful Mediterranean beach on a hot summer day and there are hundreds of people on the sand, but nobody in the water, you're not going to jump into the water. You'll think: jellyfish, sharks, toxic waste, rip tide... I mean, there's something wrong there, so you're not going to jump in! Go to the same beach when dozens of people are frolicking in the waves and you'll jump in without thinking twice. It's the same for a prospective entrepreneur.

For a young Italian graduate from a good school, given the option between a job with Telecom Italia or going towards a start-up, it would be a no brainer: they'd go for the certain job. Why? Because, until we started the programme of Partnership for Growth, few people could identify even a handful of young Italian entrepreneurs who'd left good jobs to start [successful] companies.

> *Take risk, experiment, accept failure, focus on what, why and how without neglecting economics, ecosystem dynamics and people dreams.*

Chris Lonchampt (Innovation strategist and DesignGov board member)

The rules are the easy things to think of, tangible things; the intangible, which are the hardest to quantify, are what I call 'creative chaos'. It's the ability to stand out and have that be socially acceptable.

Richard Florida did a book [*The Great Reset*] on innovation centres. One of the things he noted was: do you have open and vibrant gay and lesbian communities? Is that kind of diversity acceptable within the society? If it is, that's an indicator of [a] willingness to embrace the difference; and that's what you need to be wildly creative.

Perhaps particular societies also have less freedom to fail. That may also be quite important in deciding to be an innovative entrepreneur.

I think that's a huge challenge in Europe. In Germany, when you go bankrupt it's a pretty serious and lasting stigma. Americans are allowed [to] fail and try again. And it's part of our DNA.

Many of our forefathers were chased onto the boat from Europe because it was the debtor's prison or go to the US. We didn't want to recreate that environment here, so there's a much higher threshold for failure. Not abusive failure, not somebody who's stealing. But somebody who works hard and takes a risk and, through no fault of their own – they read the market wrong or somebody else got to the marketplace before them – that failure, in a place like Silicon Valley, is actually a badge of honour.

In government, not so much.

For many years you've been involved in promoting the case for commercial diplomacy by doing things like launching the Global Entrepreneurship Programme while you were the NSA fellow at the Hoover Institution at Stanford. Do you think it's essential to play a part in lifting the Majority World up to a higher standard of living?

Definitely. I try to make a distinction between two really important parts of growing the economy globally.

There's micro credit, which I see as the first rung on the ladder. That's getting people out of abject poverty and into being able to feed their family. But it's very rare that any of those micro-credit companies or businesses scale up. Scalable entrepreneurship creates a vibrant middle class of people who don't want to run businesses but want to be paid employees at somebody else's business.

I think entrepreneurship is wonderful but it's not for everybody. Not everybody has the risk tolerance, passion, ideas, drive or background to do that. That's why we need creative risk takers to have an ecosystem in which they can scale up and grow a business that becomes an anchor for the local community, provides good paying jobs and helps grow the middle class.

I think maybe 40 countries would be appropriate for trying to launch scalable entrepreneurship programmes – they have enough internal capital [and a] diverse and educated population [without] wholesale corruption.

How do you see innovation affecting the world economy and economics?

I believe that we're going to start seeing some high-impact, low-cost innovations. We've already seen it coming out of what, traditionally, has been thought of as the developing world. The global leader in mobile money is Kenya, partially because they don't have encumbrance in the way.

Encumbrance can be a huge barrier to innovation. And, if you've got large credit card companies and large banks arm-in-arm, it's hard to move to a purely digital, phone-based, value transfer that bypasses banks. But, that's kind of what happened in Kenya. That kind of innovation is hard for people here [in the US] to conceive of; people are so rooted in thinking that banks or credit cards have to be party to that transaction.

Innovation brings people new experiences, which will change their everyday lives as well as define the next century.
Atsufumi Yokoi (Co-founder and President of Akira Foundation)

Another thing you can think of is in healthcare. Healthcare costs in the United States [are] way out of control. You could imagine some innovations coming out of India that did 95 percent of what US processes would do, at one-tenth the cost.

It was recently reported by the Pew Institute that internet users were twice as likely to attend a political meeting, 78 percent more likely to try and influence someone's vote, and 53 percent more likely to have voted or at least intended to vote. How do you see the evolution of social platforms enhancing communication between citizens and government, local, state, federal and frankly internationally, as we become more global citizens?

It is huge. It really challenges people who're not digital natives to understand this tsunami of technology and its impact on how societies can organize themselves and respond quickly.

Look at the response to the Haiti disaster and earthquake. They were able to receive messages, translated [by crowdsourcing] from Creole to English and get 'boots on the ground' in a turnaround time of about two hours. Government would never be able to do that. It takes passionate free agents who're willing to work 24/7 and are willing and able to innovate in a way that's not bound by the bureaucracy of process. That's very empowering. If we [government] don't embrace it, we [run] the risk of becoming less relevant.

> *I've collected hundreds of definitions, and they fall into two camps. You either believe that 'invention' and 'innovation' are two separate processes that require technology transfer, or you believe that 'invention' is the first and integral stage of 'innovation'. I subscribe to the second – this is a more holistic, systemic and systematic view of the process.*
>
> *Knowledge Innovation® embodies the concept that innovation is the one competence needed for the future. It addresses all the fundamental management dimensions in the process of innovation – the creation and conversion of ideas into viable commercial products in addition to building a foundation for future sustainable growth. It recognizes that knowledge is the core component of innovation – not technology or finances per se.*
>
> *Nurturing and managing the flow of knowledge may be the most distinctive competence of the decade. Note that it operates on all three economic levels simultaneously: micro- (enterprise), meso- (nation/region economy) and macro-economic (global/societal).*
>
> **Debra Amidon** (Author and ENTOVATION founder/CEO)

Keyword imagination exercise

Take a few minutes to close your eyes, relax and explore these keywords. You may want to make a note of any ideas that emerge that you want to explore later.

Barrier, Creative, Knowledge, Solution, Talent

Suvi Linden

Finland's Minister of Communication from 2007 to 2011, Minister of Culture from 1999 to 2002 and a Member of Parliament from 1995 to 2011, Suvi Linden is Commissioner of the United Nations Broadband Commission for Digital Development and ITU's Special Envoy for the Commission. She was nominated 'Visionary of the Year' by Intelligent Community Forum 2011 and is founder and CEO of PearIcon Ltd.

You were a Member of Parliament in Finland for over 15 years. Now that you are out of party politics, do you feel more empowered to get your message across?

I have found that my position as a Special Envoy for the Broadband Commission for Digital Development gives me the prestige and status to promote things that, if I were in politics, I would not always have the possibility to do. I have very much enjoyed having the time to join conferences and discussions. When you are a minister you are just taken to the podium, where you give your speech, and then taken some-where else. Now I have the possibility to really take part and get involved. It's like a big puzzle and you get new pieces all the time because things are evolving so fast.

What was the first piece of the puzzle that made you realize that broadband was something you were passionate about and were willing to put energy towards?

I studied computer science in university. When I was Finland's Minister of Culture – from 1999 to 2002 – I wanted to promote digital content. At that time the area was still new, even in my Ministry. There weren't many experts in this field. I felt that we really needed to concentrate on information society issues, such as digital content, as I saw its potential to create new jobs and small businesses.

I was privileged to work with Information Society issues [as Chair of the Advisory Board] and, as a member of the Committee for the Future and Chair of the Education and Culture Committee. All these positions were important for me in building the vision of an information society.

I was very enthusiastic to become Finland's Minister of Communications (from 2007 until 2011) as I could use all the knowledge I had gained in the years prior to that. The communication field had many familiar faces: broadcasters, digital content producers, developers of the information society. So, in a way, the playing field was quite familiar and, quite soon, my mission became clear: I really felt that telecommunications infrastructure should be accessible all over Finland. It's the key issue to increase productivity, accessibility and efficiency for public sector services and create new opportunities for businesses in Finland.

Because of Nokia our country's mobile networks are very advanced and Finns are used to being mobile. But I understood that we had various regions in the country that have 'white spots', meaning they had no quality access to the internet. Because of that, the government decided that by 2015 we should have 100 megabyte/second high-speed access for everyone in Finland; it was a long term plan. In the short term, 1 megabyte/second access was made a legal right for everyone. We are still the only country where high quality, affordable internet access is a right by legislation.

We made a national broadband strategy that has a roadmap determining how to use public money for high-speed connection. At the time many people wondered what they would do with 100 megabyte access; markets for e-services and e-content were not, at that time, very advanced. The development of new devices that increase data transfer has been very fast; the future is smartphones, tablets, mobile networks and 4G.

It's not only mobile or only fibre: it's both together. Good fibre networks are necessary, and that will take time and a lot of money – both public and private. Governments should have the vision and a strategy as to how to accomplish it.

We have seen in Australia, for instance, that in rural areas a good connection is the most important asset, if you want to have businesses and jobs there; it's for education... it's for all kinds of thing. In Europe we are used to having a very strong public sector, and the public sector is responsible for many services. I think communication technology – broadband – is a very important tool to be able to provide these public services in a more efficient, productive way. Statistics show that 50 percent of the growth in productivity in the private sector has been due to use of communication technology.

My new mission is focused on communities and municipalities. Local politicians should have a digital agenda looking at all the different sectors – health, education, environment, technical – and make a roadmap showing how, by changing the current way of doing things and by using ICT, they can be more productive and efficient. It is important for politicians to have an overall view and understanding of the cost of ICT investments as well as the return on investment.

In a city of this kind, where ICT is really well used, the benefits include, for instance, elderly people being able to stay longer and more safely at home with the help of communication technology.

Do you think that broadband should be part of the common wealth of a nation – and a free government service – much like roads are; or should it be run as a 'for profit' business?

I believe that the private sector should be the investor in the networks. The cost of using these networks should be affordable. The government's role is to ensure that the regulations and business environment are good; expensive auctions for spectrum allocations are an obstacle for private investments.

Unfortunately too often governments have seen the telecommunication field as a good way to get money for the state budget. The challenge for the government is to understand that telecommunication networks are a long-term investment for the future of the country and economic growth.

The digital society is the most important tool for economic growth and the government should be an enabler. So I like to explain to politicians that instead of having high-level auctions for frequency allocation they should really create an enabling environment, with good regulation, so that everyone can benefit – citizens, businesses and the government.

Do you think that broadband connectivity enables innovation and innovative thought?

Of course. When we had our economic crisis in Finland in the 1990s, the government decided to put a lot of money into R&D. That's when Nokia was developing and researching mobile radio technology, and they soon became the biggest mobile phone manufacturer in the world. Now we are facing the challenge of finding new areas for innovations. I'm quite optimistic that we can do it in Finland.

> *If there is one trait that helped me land top positions in public and private finance, break glass ceilings and land on the international speaking circuit without any prior experience it boils down to one thing: innovation.*
> **Noor Aftab** (Author, speaker, business adviser and disruptive innovator)

I notice that you're a member of an online group called Girls in ICT Portal; and you've said, 'The future is made in the field of ICT and there should be more women present.' Do you think the fact that there isn't a balanced representation of women in ICT in some way affects how young women approach innovative industries?

I think that at the beginning the ICT industry was very engineering oriented; it is still the case that technology is essential but, more and more, content and apps are ruling the markets. Girls and women can play very strong roles in the development of user-friendly apps and digital content, though they'll still need to understand communication technology to be part of the team combining the technology and user-friendly interfaces.

I strongly believe that if we can make young girls understand that mathematics and physics need to be part of their studies if they want to be able to do exciting things with ICT, then I think there will be more girls in ICT. Even though I studied computer science I'm not an engineer, but I am crazy about information technology and its power to change the world!

> *Innovation is too often considered as a binary thing – we are/are not innovative. Looking at innovation in these absolute terms is a mistake. Innovation is a feature or characteristic that can be developed through an allocation of appropriate resources – personnel time, company project budgets, government funding. Constrained resources can then be allocated on a basis of promoting innovation as a significant and recurrent feature of an organization, rather than as an absolute condition to be achieved. Allocation is imperative as it requires a positive action with direct respect to the pursuit of innovation. Too often, companies and governments hope that innovation is a happy by-product of other activities.*

The greatest barrier to success is where this allocation is a conditional one, for example where a government's level of innovation funding depends on a range of variables such as economic performance so that the worse the performance, the less support is made available for innovation. There is overwhelming evidence that a lack of commitment to a sustained level of innovation support will greatly inhibit outcomes. Innovation needs a stable environment where the forward commitment of resources can be relied upon. The failure of companies, governments and the like to maintain their commitments to their allocations can be the greatest barrier to the success of any innovation programme.

Kris Gale (Managing Partner of Michael Johnson Associates)

Keyword imagination exercise

Access, Broadband, Involved, Network, Women

Peter Cochrane

Peter Cochrane is an adviser and consultant to governments and companies. He has worked in circuit, system and network design; software, human interfaces and programming; adaptive systems; AI and AL; company transformation and management. Peter was formerly CTO of BT and has also been the Collier Chair for the Public Understanding of Science and Technology at Bristol, a visiting Professor to CNET, Southampton, Nottingham Trent, Robert Gordon's, Kent, Essex and University College London. He has received numerous awards including the C&G Prince Philip Medal, the IEEE Millennium Medal, an OBE, the Queen's Award for Innovation and The Martlesham Medal.

You've noted that you believe the greatest barrier to the success of innovation is people. Do you think people can be trained to be more open to innovation or is it just about them getting out of the way so innovation can succeed?

Fundamentally, human beings do not like change. No matter what the change is, they balk at it. It doesn't matter what you do, or try to do – people will object.

I'll give you an example. We've had public inquiry after public inquiry about nuclear power [in the UK]; for at least the last 30 years. Engineers and planners have been leaping up and down at government, telling them that the lights are going to go out. In three years' time, we'll [have] rolling blackouts in the UK; and the big decisions on building power stations will come for a very simple reason: people won't be able to watch 'Neighbours' or 'EastEnders'. That's all it will take; all the debate will disappear.

What they don't understand is, it takes 5 to 10 years to build a power station. And so this country will soon be standing on the brink of being plunged into some second-world status because it hasn't got enough power. Production will go down, GDP will go down. Moreover, some of the best companies in the UK will not be able to operate without 24/7 power, so some of those will leave the UK. A lot of people who are trying to do business here, like me, can't operate without power – so we'll pick up sticks and leave.

> *The greatest impediment to the success of innovation is the pomposity of organizations.*
> **Nicholas Gruen** (Chairman of the Australian Centre for Social Innovation)

Now you've got a really interesting situation with political minds that are worried about staying in power, limited by some idiotic ideology laid down in the 1920s during the Industrial Revolution of old: a focus on social programmes, giving people a good standard of living and having a dependency culture. Who pays for it? Business does. But business can't work if you're dead in the water. And so, for various reasons, the likelihood is that we're going to suffer. It's not unique: America's going in the same direction.

Go to Southeast Asia and every country you go to has a vision, a mission and a plan. They know what they want to be when they grow up. Only one nation in the Western college of countries has actually got a vision, a mission and a plan, and that's Germany. The UK and US don't. France doesn't, Italy doesn't, Spain doesn't. Ergo, they're in a mess.

You've clarified 'the problem' as you see it; but I'm not sure if, at this stage, you see a solution.

It sounds crude, but when a critical mass of all the technophobes and the tech-ignorant people in society have gone and been replaced by tech-savvy youngsters, the problem will go away. I am not being brutal. It just seems to be a simple fact of life. Some of the best managerial change programmes that we've engaged in have come about because the critical mass of negative people, or people who don't understand, have retired.

Like my husband and I, you and your wife, Jane, work together. Is that a situation that works well for you?

It works extremely well. Sometimes women get upset with me when I say this, but: women are absolutely different to men. They think differently and therein lies their great value. If you give men and women a problem, very often they will come to a sensible solution by entirely different routes. That's incredibly powerful.

No matter how bright you are, no matter how good you are in your given field, without somebody to balance ideas out you can get yourself in a mental cul-de-sac. A man and wife can say things to each other and be honest in ways that you couldn't be, necessarily, with an employee – although I have worked with some pretty remarkable women in my life. Jane knows what I'm thinking before I think it, you know – wives do. So she makes contributions that no one else could.

> *Innovation is not some new product or service: it's a path, which a company chooses in order to compete successfully in the future. Of course, a single piece of innovation, or a cluster, is related to a minor/major change or improvement in products, processes or services. However, each of these innovative pieces should be aligned with corporate/government vision and strategy. Hence, innovative clusters become not just a standalone new product but form a foundation for further business growth and the societal development.*
> **Yaroslav Baronov** (Co-founder of RO-BO.ru and Emociy.ru)

Keyword imagination exercise

GDP, Mission, Plan, Vision, Wife

Simon Sheikh

Simon Sheikh was the National Director of GetUp, Australia's leading online political advocacy organization from 2008 to 2012. He is running for the Australian Senate, representing the Greens Party, in the 2013 federal election.

Photo credit: Courtney Tight

Do you see innovation as an imperative?

As progressivists, people with progressive values, we exist both to empathize with people and with the planet we live on. But we also have to challenge the status quo. And you can't challenge the status quo without accepting the need for innovation. It's crucial to us. Our belief in innovation is actually a function of the values that we hold, and I think that connection is really important.

> The biggest barrier to innovation is 'groupthink'. Too many organizations unconsciously don't want innovative new ideas that, by definition, challenge the status quo. Instead they favour a kind of groupthink where 'everyone knows' that a certain idea, process or way of doing business is the right one. And all too often if anyone challenges this accepted wisdom there are negative consequences. For many people it's much easier, safer and more comfortable to go along.
>
> **Rob Atkinson** (President of the Information Technology and Innovation Foundation)

You must also face the challenge of cynicism, which can be daunting.

Our response to cynicism is to present coherent theories of change. We take the time to explain the impact of the work that we do; we explain the context and the theory... Our optimism, as well as our belief in the theory of change, I think, protects us from the cynicism that exists in broader society.

You also enable people, via social media, to become involved in your work and often make a difference. A great example of this would be your Great Barrier Reef campaign.

That was a great campaign, where we proved that we can influence a global agenda. We [GetUp members] believe that there shouldn't be a massive coal export expansion in Australia. A side effect of this expansion is that we'd trash our Great Barrier Reef. This would happen directly as a result of the extra 10,000 ships going through the reef; and indirectly as a result of the extra carbon emissions that, obviously, impact coral bleaching through the ocean temperatures.

So, GetUp put the Great Barrier Reef on one side of this campaign that we were fighting and we put the coal barons, Clive Palmer and Gina Rinehart, on the other side. They were the people who are responsible for the plan, which has now been knocked over, to build the world's largest coal export facility right on the coast of the Great Barrier Reef.

How important do you feel the GetUp movement is to making change?

Our model has its constraints, so we work best in partnership with established organizations that have a deeper policy knowledge and have been in the game for a long period of time. They have the political relationships.

So, would you say your work is determined by political parties or political organizations?

Our challenge is to create a progressive Australia. And Australia will never be a progressive country, and never have its progressive balance protected, until all political parties accept the types of values that we hold to be true.

In 10 years' time, what do you hope you'll be able to say about the GetUp movement?

I think the moment we're in, in Australia – which is different from the moment we're in globally – is: we're seeing technologies starting to scale beyond being used by one side of politics, one organization, or one group of people, with a certain value set. Therefore, I hope what we can say is that we were successful in embracing change and innovation. I hope we look back at this moment and say, 'We were open to being innovative innovators – not just innovators, full stop.'

> *I'm working on a concept called People's Cabinet which (in its most basic form) asks the question: who would Australians choose to be Commonwealth Government Cabinet Ministers if they got to vote for these positions, rather than simply for their local members? The goal of the tool is to educate people about our political system and individual parliamentarians and to give citizens a voice in stating their preferences for Ministers. It has a lot of iterations and potential uses within the political and commercial spheres.*

Craig Thomler (Managing Director of Delib Australia)

Keyword imagination exercise

Constraints, Embrace, Empathize, Impact, Values

Robert Jacobson

Robert Jacobson is CEO, co-founder, Chairman and Strategist at Atelier Tomorrow based in San Francisco and Malmö, Sweden. A lifelong student of human experience, Robert is an expert on innovation-management issues, especially the development of regional innovation platforms that produce continuous social and technological innovation.

Your company name is intriguing: Atelier Tomorrow… where did the idea for that come from?

Artists of the Renaissance often lived and worked with their student-helps. You might have six of the greatest painters in history working right next to each other, each in his or her studio, looking over their shoulders, each watching what the other guy was doing, borrowing ideas, tweaking each other's inventions… collaborating! Ateliers were the Skunk Works of the past.

We chose 'Tomorrow' because we're creating an atelier for the future. We're coming up with new ways of envisioning and then realizing remarkable futures in prosaic situations: the household, the urban development, in offices, etc. We're learning to design innovation platforms, environments and situations where social and technological innovation can be made continuous.

What makes our work unique is our corollary focus on the mixing zone where virtual worlds and the physical worlds conjoin. How can you craft designs for business, residential and mixed-use environments that encompass the experience of the intangible, pervasive, omnipresent, multidimensional flow of information, knowledge, education and entertainment that permeates the development? This is a new challenge. It's the sort of problem on which we thrive.

One of our larger projects (in terms of geography), the Nordic Clearinghouse for Service Innovation, will create a vast trans-Nordic emporium of information, knowledge and experiences related to service innovation – also places to interact with that knowledge and to collaborate across organizational and national boundaries. An online bazaar.

> *What corporates can learn from how start-ups innovate fascinates me. I think the future of consultancy will shift from just giving advice and move into co-venturing with clients.*
> **Philippe De Ridder** (Founder of Board of Innovation)

Another project, yet untitled, applies similar principles to enable people in maritime cities and those far from the sea to experience water in their own lives, on the seashore, in the harbour and in rivers and streams. This is in anticipation of next year's promotion by the European Commission – the EU's executive organ – of the concept of Blue Growth, a European Commission project which begins in 2014. The EC is consolidating its research, development activities, certain projects and their departments into four super-directorates. One of these is going to be for maritime and marine affairs. Its goal is to optimize the use of maritime and marine resources to drive economic prosperity on the land.

Scandinavian countries have a high level of social involvement in endeavours such as these. Do you think the models you're able to take advantage of, within the Scandinavian region, can apply to larger economies like the United States and China, or do you think they will remain exclusively high-value Scandinavian concepts?

Part of the motivation for undertaking these projects is to highlight and export to the rest of the world Nordic expertise, capacity for innovation and values including service to and respect for the community and nature.

We've also a concern for the region's place in the world. Small-economy regions like Scandinavia will be at the mercy of large-economy regions like Asia and North America unless they take their destinies into their own hands.

Thus our largest challenge is to be able to create global 'zones of awareness' that can level the playing field by communicating desirable values. Every country has an interest in ensuring that its residents are informed and in accord with its national purpose, whatever that may be. But what about the world at large, in which all of us are citizens? Who speaks for it? We hope to create grassroots networks of communication that engender continuous global sharing of information, ideas and values.

The closest the world comes to that ideal today is the Olympics: suddenly the whole world is connected and billions are watching… and just as suddenly, they go away! We want to create online places where the world's citizens are able to interact and deal with both local issues and with global grand challenges – like climate change – that affect us all. We want to help to create opportunities for communication, collaboration and responsibly living together that won't go away.

> *The cornerstones of innovation are design, technology, usability and obsolescence. And there is only one success metric – 'enriching the psychological wellbeing of users, while creating positive societal value'. For innovation to become the order of the day, we need to discard every remnant of the Industrial Age thought process. Sustained value from innovation will only come by creating a culture first and culture is both subjective and contextual.*
>
> **Sunil Malhotra** (Founder and Head of Creative Culture at Ideafarms)

Keyword imagination exercise

Future, Interact, Problem, Opportunity, Responsibility

Gustav Praekelt

Gustav Praekelt is the founder and CEO of the Praekelt Group and the Praekelt Foundation. He is a thought leader in the fields of mobile platforms, technology and services and solutions for Majority World initiatives, which have reached over 50 million people in 15 African countries.

What was the impetus for you starting the Praekelt Foundation?

I think that comes down to your Foundation Question: 'How do you define innovation?' which actually floored me for a while. I realized that I really see it as prescribing solutions to problems that people face in their day-to-day lives. If there's something small that we can do to solve these problems, we can have a really large impact.

I think that's my personal creed: to effect large-scale change with simple, parsimonious, lean interventions. There are simple things we can do with mobile technology that don't necessarily cost a lot of money, which we can do on a large scale. That probably defines why we started the non-profit.

It's the manifestation of frugal innovation.

Exactly.

You work in the arena of mobile telephony, a technology that is having a tremendous impact on your continent. What is your vision for how mobile technology can transform Africa in general and South Africa in particular?

It's the fastest growing technological evolution of mankind. Faster than television, radio, books, the printing press, anything like that. In 20 years we've gone from zero to 6 billion people having mobile phones.

It's the first time in the history of humankind that we have a mechanism to communicate with almost every living human on the planet in a cost-effective way. The challenge is: what we do with this incredible tool that we've been given?

I think inequality is at the root of all the problems in South Africa right now... the vast difference in income people have in this country. The question is: how do we make people's lives better and have a more equitable distribution of wealth and information?

> *The way innovation works for me is to, essentially, step back from the project and look at it as if I've never seen it before. Innovation is really taking what works in one space and applying it to another. I take that approach to thinking, too. I'll look at a problem and say: if everyone else approaches this problem from door number one, what happens if we look at it from door number three? It's a deliberate fragmentation of a problem into pieces that can be reassembled in almost any way you want.*
>
> **Maggie Fox** (Founder, CEO and Chief Marketing Officer of the Social Media Group)

A lot of the problems that we face in Africa, and in the Majority World, can be regressed through the delivery of information and service. Quite often the privation of illness is not necessarily the treatment of illness; a lot can be done by providing the correct information at the right time. Diarrhoea is the largest cause of infant mortality in the Majority World at the moment. So, getting people to hand-wash properly causes a dramatic decrease in the incidents of diarrhoea, which then causes a decrease in infant mortality. It's the same thing with information on the transmission of HIV/AIDS or how to prevent the transmission to children. Most of that information is transferral, and we know that almost everybody's got a device, so we can communicate with them.

If mobile connectivity in the developing world is almost ubiquitous, what is the state of mobile data infrastructure and how do you see that moving forward?

[All] GSM networks have at least GPRS technology data and most of them have 3G data, so, the infrastructure isn't really so much of a problem. If you map availability of mobile network infrastructure in Africa versus the availability of electrical infrastructure, mobile is about three to four times more available than electricity, which is incredible. I think something like 90 to 95 percent of the population of the continent of Africa can have a data connection. So, data infrastructure is 'won and done'.

The next step is how to make it affordable, and that can be broken into two issues. One is the cost of the handset, as data-capable handsets are still fairly expensive. Smart phones are just touching on $50 now. I think this is a magical point, at which a family, even a family living on $2 a day can say, 'Our investment in this phone is worth our while for the benefits that will accrue from being connected and being able to buy data.' So, let's say that's close on being solved.

Now, if you ask somebody who lives in a rural area or slum, for instance, they might have a feature phone capable of using data. But, if you ask them if they are using data every day, they'd say, 'Oh, not really.' Why? It's not because they're illiterate, or that they're not aware there is data; it's because they can't accurately calculate how much it will cost to use in a single session.

They know if they send an SMS it will cost exactly 1 shilling or 5 shillings or whatever the rate might be, in whatever currency. The problem is, if you're using data at the moment, flat rate data is not available for the base of the pyramid. They worry that they may only have 50 or 100 shillings in their data or mobile account and, by going to Facebook, they might be using it up. All of a sudden, they don't have airtime available to call their mother or son for life-saving information.

We have a lot of work to do as network operators and service providers to solve that problem. We can see the glimmers of hope in things like

Wikipedia Zero [which enables access to Wikipedia, without data charges, in some developing nations] and 0.facebook.com. That's one solution; the other is that network operators are coming up with capped, flat-rate charges.

It's very apparent that you are extremely focused on empowering the Majority World. And the numbers there are astronomical. Once that empowerment happens, the effect on the Global Digital Economy could be exponential.

The Majority World is where the majority of the world's population is, where the majority of the interesting problems lie and, potentially, where the profits lie. We think the Majority World is where the most interesting things are going to happen in this century; that obviously includes Africa, South America, Latin America and Asia Pacific.

When we build services we don't just target the base of pyramid, we target a geographic area. For instance, if we build a music service or a health service, we don't just target the very poorest people: we target everybody in Africa or everybody in Nigeria or Kenya. We think of it as Majority World services. The GDP growth in Africa is, on average, 6–7 percent, and I think that all the evidence shows that this century is going to be the century of the Majority World.

But, purely from a personal perspective, I'm interested in empowering people. It's a personal mission of mine; and, as a non-profit, we think just by connecting people and allowing them to pursue their own goals by using mobile technologies, we will see an incredible explosion in information, services and the creation of wealth.

It seems to me that if you have a great amount of resources to hand, innovation may not be an overriding imperative.

I definitely believe that. I'm a firm believer in parsimonious engineering or frugal innovation.

Constraints drive innovation. Resource-constraints mean that people go and find interesting solutions to work around all those constraints. That's why so many of the interesting innovations in mobile, and mobile payments, come out of Africa.

I think there's going to be a huge explosion in innovation in civil society, collaborative government and open government. A lot of those things are going to come to fruition within Africa, simply because we have such obstacles to overcome. Certainly many of the innovations in [e-]health are being driven in Africa.

> *I want people, including people who don't have technical skills, to be able to use and repurpose CrowdVoice to empower their own movements by improving the way they collect and disseminate knowledge about specific human rights causes. It is an open source platform that tracks voices of protest from around the world by curating information and crowdsourcing valuable data – whether it's eyewitness videos, images, blogs or news reports – in order to facilitate the spread of knowledge on current social justice movements worldwide. It's important for this information to be accessible and easily discovered, especially in an age where we have so much censorship. It's a step forward in creating a global community from civic engagement.*
>
> **Esra'a al Shafei** (TED Senior Fellow, Founder and Director of Mideast Youth and crowdvoice.org)

The implications of how OpenGov or Gov 2.0 could affect the continent are staggering!

It's just incredible, I promise you! If you think about what government really is, or is supposed to be… why do we pay taxes? We pay taxes because we want a stable environment. The lack of a truly representational government is, quite often, a logistical problem. Mobile could take that problem away. In the next 5 to 10 years it's going to be really interesting to see what's going to happen in the Majority World when people realize that they have this direct power to influence government.

I think a lot of that innovation is going to happen from local government. For example, walking around my community, by pointing my phone at a bridge I could find out who paid for it… backhanders that got paid… who is responsible. Or looking at anything that's broken in your community; there's a pothole or a streetlamp that's not working: you point your camera and… take a picture of it and that goes into a trouble-ticketing system for your local government.

On the other side, I think there's going to be a huge revolution regarding distribution of wealth. Because, when we look at the Majority World what characterizes it is not too much poverty but an over-abundance of certain types of resource and a lack of resources in other areas. A lot of problems that we have in the Majority World are based on logistical problems and the flow of information, more so than real abject poverty. Certainly, Africa is capable of feeding itself. There's enough food being produced but we've got logistical [problems]. So, I think, a really interesting space for innovation is going to be how do we exchange value? How do we mediate a more equitable distribution of wealth and services? This is definitely the continent where you want to be, because we're going to see a mind-blowing change.

> *Global Minimum, an organization which I co-founded over six years ago, recently launched Innovate Salone – the first ever high school innovation challenge in Sierra Leone. The Innovate Salone platform gives young people the opportunity to impact and enhance community at a local level to promote larger national development. Through these networks and relationships, I believe Sierra Leone will usher in a new wave of doers who will transform their society.*
> **David Moinina Sengeh** (Graduate student, PhD candidate at MIT (MIT Media Lab) and co-founder of Global Minimum and Lebone)

Keyword imagination exercise

Affordable, Data, Distribution, GDE, Influence

Tiago Peixoto

Tiago Peixoto is a world-renowned expert on digital democracy specializing in online participatory budgeting and wiki-legislation. An open government specialist in the ICT4Gov programme of the World Bank Institute's Open Governance cluster, Tiago has worked as a policy adviser for organizations such as the OECD, the UN and the Brazilian and UK governments, and has been involved in pioneering e-Gov initiatives in Africa, Asia, Europe, Latin America and the Caribbean. Among other publications, Tiago is co-author of the *2010 United Nations e-Government Survey: Leveraging e-government at a time of financial and economic crisis*; he is also research coordinator of the Electronic Democracy Centre in Zurich.

One of your areas of expertise is Gov 2.0; what specific initiatives are you currently focusing on?

One is what I am calling 'online-to-offline innovation' and the second is the idea of cross-selling and up-selling in the public sector.

In the online Gov 2.0 (electronic government) world, it is natural to imitate whatever is done in the offline world. For instance, if people vote offline you want to think of a way to do online voting. So, we're normally thinking of ways to innovate in terms of transferring procedures from the offline to the online world; ie if you pay your bills offline, now you can start to pay your bills online.

At the same time, there are lots of things happening in the online world that are online inventions. For instance, budget data visualizations, like those from the Open Knowledge Foundation, are easy ways to visualize data – they're user-friendly and accessible to the normal citizen. In the same way we're trying to get things from the offline world and repeat them in the online world, there are a number of innovations happening now in the online world that we may want to enact offline as well. So, for instance, right now we start to see budget visualizations – originally conceived online – being painted in street walls. This type of 'reversed engineering' may be one of the most promising things in the coming years, and we are just touching the surface of it.

The second idea I call 'cross-selling in the public sector'. For instance, when you go to Amazon and you buy a book, they try to sell you other books. That's traditional cross-selling; they try to get lots of information about you and how you've been behaving so they can offer you something else. If you call a bank, they will eventually give you the service that you want, but not before they've tried to sell you insurance or a new plan. The private sector has been successfully doing this for years but, amazingly, the public sector never does it. In the public sector, if a citizen calls we just give the information requested, or do whatever transaction is supposed to happen, and then hang up the phone.

At the same time, governments are coming to people like me and saying, 'Can we create a platform to do crowdsourcing?' Then, when they create the crowdsourcing platform, nobody comes. All the while, they're getting a million calls a day from citizens – often from extremely hard to reach constituencies – interacting with them, but they're hanging up the phone too soon.

> *I'm focused on helping revitalize downtown Vegas, which includes downtownproject.com. One of the goals is to make downtown Vegas the most community-focused large city in the world, and another goal is to help inspire other cities to focus on becoming more community-focused as a way to revitalize themselves.*
> **Tony Hsieh** (best-selling author, entrepreneur, instigator of innovation and initiator of the Las Vegas' Downtown Project)

They've got a universe of people calling, so when they call, give them the service that they want; but, at the end of the call, why not ask: 'How can we improve government in your area?' or, 'How many power cuts did you get last week? Does your trash get collected every day?' or, 'What is your perception of corruption in your area?' and so on. You can cross-sell participation to some extent.

You can create channels of interaction to collect data from citizens who are interacting with government. The idea is to use these existing channels of interaction to gather feedback to create citizen-generated data, which is distributed intelligence at its best. With this data, you can create analytics and amazing tools to assist in decision making – all by cross-selling relationships and participation.

Are some nations more open to e-Gov, or Gov 2.0, than others?

Let's look at some developed countries that are doing great things when it comes to e-Gov, for instance the countries that have been doing internet voting, online referenda and crowdsourcing constitutions. There are lots of initiatives in Switzerland, Iceland, Estonia, Norway, Sweden and so on. What these countries have in common is a high level of connectivity, a high level of trust in institutions and they're extremely small countries.

The other day I had talks with [Google CEO] Eric Schmidt and with Toomas Ilves, the President of Estonia. They were two separate conversations, but they both spoke about identity and authentication as being huge issues when looking at online innovation in government issues. But, once you get them right, it's extremely easy to do.

Estonia and Switzerland, for instance, are small countries with a high level of connectivity, which makes it easier to implement online authentication systems. It's a totally different thing to try and implement that in Australia or the United States – which have different federal and state laws, etc. Smaller countries are more able to roll out online authentication processes, which may lead to more innovation in terms of online democratic participation.

The other thing is, in nascent – recent – democracies, democracy is not a matter of procedure. You normally have to create a new constitutional framework and you may be more prone to experimenting. For example, you'll see lots of experimentation in democracy in Latin American countries that come out of periods of dictatorship. But it is not surprising: they have to start building democracy from zero.

At the same time there is a democratic malaise in the 'outside' world where people are thinking: why not try something different? Some of these experiments will die, others survive. It's an evolutionary approach to democratic innovation. This evolutionary approach is much more likely to exist in emerging democracies where people have a blank slate to start deciding how they want things to be done.

Have you any thoughts as to how innovation and innovative tools in general, and e-Gov in particular, might assist in moving the EU forward and out of its current malaise?

Before getting into that answer, let's be clear: I am a person who works with technology, but there are some kinds of tech we should avoid.

Let me tell you a quick story. Right after the French Revolution, the optic telegraph was invented; also called the Napoleonic telegraph. It sent messages via lights that were relayed across towers. People thought there would be a huge revolution in the way democracy and institutions worked. There were lots of very smart people writing about it, just like nowadays, saying things that sound a lot like what we are saying nowadays. And none of the things they wrote and talked about happened, because government change is institutional change. Technology just follows. Technology is not as disruptive in the way governments work – in the public sector – as it is in the private sector.

So this brings me to the EU, where I've seen excitement around technology – and lots of EU funds going into it – year after year. The first problem – which is in the EU but is also in the entire technology-in-government space – is that every time there's a new buzzword, we forget everything that we've learnt and practised. The first way for innovation to be effective in this space is to remember that knowledge is cumulative – so we can stop repeating the same mistakes.

That said, there's one extremely interesting thing about the EU that is totally different from, for instance, the United States or Australia. In the EU, you have extremely different governmental arrangements. In some places the government is centralized, in other places it's federal; in some places the [Prime] minister may call most of the shots, while in other cases you have more collaborative types of government. There is such a high level of diversity, in terms of arrangements and how organizations work, that the EU is a living lab. Because of this, you can have much more trial and error, which is the source of innovation.

In many ways, your description of the variances within the EU reminded me of the CARICOM economic zone – the Caribbean Single Market and Economy (CSME). It's an area of the world that is really interesting because the various national populations are, in general, very well educated, they're doing their best to be as technologically forward as possible, and they are influenced, to varying degrees, by South America, Britain and the US. To my mind, it too is a living lab.

Actually, what you've said is very interesting. We have small nations, which makes experimentation and leverage in experimentation much easier because it's controllable; the costs are fewer and much more controllable; and the costs of implementation are lower – even though they're relatively high, there's a difference.

There is also a huge level of institutional variance. Some administrations, such as those in the Ultramar territories, like in Guadalupe, function according to the French administrative style; then you have some, like Barbados, that have a more Anglo-Saxon administration; you have the Dutch in Aruba, and then nations like the Dominican Republic, which are a mixture. The biggest problem there, apart from all the governance problems – such as corruption, which is endemic – is their connectivity. But as connectivity increases, it's definitely a place to be looking. It's worth thinking about CARICOM as a 'small Europe', but with a much higher level of diversity, particularly culturally.

It is a microcosm that is fascinating. The question is: to what extent will the region, and it's leaders, be prone to innovation? Innovation is likely to happen everywhere, but what is interesting is watching the 'trial and error' that leads to innovation. To what extent, I wonder, will this trial be allowed to happen in the Caribbean?

> *Innovation is the culmination of creativity, art and collaboration for the betterment of society and is a vehicle for government and business.*
>
> **Dan Mathieson** (Mayor of 'Smart City' Stratford, Ontario, Canada)

Final thoughts

Innovation is changing nations, some to degrees that were unimaginable only a handful of years ago. Those nations, and leaders, that have a clear strategy that empowers their citizens are likely to have a bright future. Those who do not adapt may be at the mercy of the globalization, enhanced by innovative tools, techniques and technologies, which has taken root in recent years. Among the many lessons to be gleaned from the Arab Spring, begun in December 2010 and continuing to this day, there are two which stand out to me. First: if the powers that be shut down the communication infrastructure for fear of hearing criticism from its citizens, citizens will take to the streets to be heard. Second: it was social media which empowered a population to organize, articulate and act at a speed that eventually left the powers that were, powerless.

It is not just dictators and despots who are affected by the power of these innovations. Through the growing transparency engendered by OpenGov and Gov 2.0 technologies and techniques, citizens of many nations are holding their elected representatives accountable over the proverbial 'pork barrel' and demanding more influence over politics, policies and services than ever before.

Flat world navigators connecting the dots

03

Art, Capability, Combine,
Cooperate, Expression, Ideas,
Jazz, Music, Partner, People, Resources,
Stability, Storytelling

Joint ventures, corporate strategies and personnel coordination are no longer limited by location. Business is already being done via innovative tools such as social media, while more and more mobile, agile innovative technologies are coming online, which will enable businesses, anywhere in the world, both large and small, to be equal competitors on the commercial playing field. It matters less and less whether a commodity is located in Sydney, San Francisco, Shanghai or São Paulo, as businesses can access virtually anything (and anyone) in any place, at any time.

Doing business has become less and less about sales executives 'mustering the troops' to 'go forth and conquer'. Instead, those people who excel at making and maintaining dynamic relationships – the 'connectors and collaborators' I characterize as Flat World Navigators

(FWNs) – will, through the use of innovative tools, techniques and technologies, carry the banner of business success across the flat world of the Global Digital Economy (GDE).

To paraphrase Pulitzer Prize winner and *NY Times* columnist Thomas Friedman, the flattening of the world happened at the dawn of the 21st century. This is a fact that countries, companies, communities, governments and individuals can, and must, adapt to. Commercially, we are moving forward and away from the eras of fierce nationalistic boundaries, empires and homogeneous companies. The ability to connect globally and cross-culturally is now a requisite for the companies and individuals looking to thrive; it will only become more so in the future.

One of the singular truths of this change in the quality and quantity of connections is that many of the former competitive advantages, enjoyed and expected by the leaders of the status quo, will no longer be exclusively available to a small circle of 'players'. This change, which countries and companies must come to grips with if they want to continue to be competitive, equates to a flat world of equal opportunity. As acknowledgement of the flat world becomes *de rigueur*, and the unprecedented potential that comes with the skilful use of innovative communication technologies becomes more fully understood and accepted by business leaders, so too will the importance of flat world navigation and FWNs be endorsed and embraced.

Almost anyone can take advantage of the opportunities inherent in the successful navigation of the flat world. This can be directly by being an FWN, or indirectly by leveraging and celebrating the skills of the FWNs within your organization. FWNs work in the new GDE, combining and leveraging both traditional and web-based technologies – such as cloud computing, social media, Web 3.0 and the semantic web – to reach out, communicate, cooperate and collaborate globally. They're often top-notch 'tweeters', usually with notable LinkedIn networks – they may even have readers beating a path to their personal blogs. FWNs have got something to say and they've found a compelling way of saying it. An effective FWN will generally have an excellent grasp of the current zeitgeist; if not on the leading edge themselves, they are connected with people – individually or through networks and communities – who can keep them up to date.

For those in sales and marketing, flat world navigating means communicating with clients and customers without the 'spin' that has often been associated with sales and marketing in the past. In the flat world, customers are too savvy to be convinced by a 'hard sell'. Due to the depth and breadth of the flat world an FWN is often involved in cross-cultural team building. This necessitates an awareness of cultural issues as well as architecting how to deal with specific and often differing cultural, company and country contexts.

The transformation that innovations to communication tools and techniques have had on the power of the enduser/consumer has enabled both the data ownership and attention economies, which are core foundations of the GDE. And, as attention is bombarded by increasing modes of media, a cold, hard fact is: it doesn't matter how good your idea or product is if people are not paying attention to it.

FWNs are the influencers who, by judicious use of these innovations, bring attention to ideas, products, services and the like. As such, their role is absolutely critical. They are the evolution of sales and marketing, embodied as a company's honest avatar. In short, they are the real-world conduit for a dialogue between the consumer and the company.

In Chapter 1 I mentioned ROI – Return On Involvement. This is where FWNs excel. For any and every organization, regardless of size or situation, be they for-profit or an NGO, leveraging the skills of their FWNs, who in turn are leveraging both traditional and innovative communication tools and techniques – is essential. How effectively this is done will be a key differentiator and, as such, must be part of a successful strategy for any organization.

Another key differentiator will be acknowledging and acting upon the fact that not only is the world becoming flatter daily but also that there are seismic demographic shifts occurring at the same time. What this means is that existing infrastructures, and the legacy of assumptions that go along with them, are no longer applicable. Rather than heavily gearing business decisions around Generation X and consumers in the West, focus will have to shift to the majority world, which must be taken seriously as a major market segment. This is also true of the millennial generation – Generation Y. The answer to the question: 'Why focus on Gen Y?' is quite simple: they are massive in number, diverse in interests, demanding in expectation, and abundantly aware that they are empowered, engaged and enabled endusers – and they expect to be treated as such.

Setting business aside for a moment, I would like to consider those young people who take their access to innovative communication tools to be as natural as their parents may have taken access to telephones and television. It can come as no surprise that there are now multiple generations of young people growing up with the ability and propensity to make friends online, in a world far wider (and yes, flatter) than anything imaginable by their parents at a comparable age. As such, their global perspective is broader, their awareness of and acceptance of other ways of life is deeper, and their tendency to believe that differences are dissatisfactory is far less demonstrable. All of these natural-born collaborators – these navigators of the flat world – will, I suggest, be far less likely to begin a war with their Facebook friends, wherever they may reside and whatever scripture they may subscribe to.

Roz Savage *Author, adventurer, environmental campaigner and world record ocean rower*

Photo credit: Elena ZhuKova

I believe in walking the talk – or rowing it. If you're trying to influence behaviour, the best thing you can do is to exemplify that behaviour, and through your own life demonstrate the benefits. Show that it's possible to be green *and* have fun. Show that you can simplify your life *and* be happier for it. In this era of hype and spin, people welcome an authentic messenger.

INTERVIEWS

Jonathan Cousins

Jonathan Cousins is co-founder of Cousins & Sears Creative Technologists. He is a designer, programmer and entrepreneur specializing in the creation of data visualizations, large-screen computational art, creative digital workflows and general software applications. His innovative work has been presented at various conferences and festivals, including the Sundance Film Festival.

How important is collaboration to your work?

Very, very important. My creative partnership with Nick Sears is hugely significant. I value it a great deal because collaborative dynamics – trust, honesty, generosity, etc – amplify your best thinking, so I see the relationship as a real intellectual achievement and professional gift.

Nick and I have a lot of interests, but one of them is very simple: we love to design, engineer and build physical things that make images. Based in part on Nick's thesis work at NYU on The Orb and the large-screen work we do for pieces like ABACUS (the one we took to Sundance) we've developed a reputation for developing both content for custom screens and for the development and design of the screens themselves. It's a business direction one could never invent from scratch, and it really brings together almost everything we've formally/academically pursued in tech and the arts – from electrical engineering to painting. In this coming year we've got several projects, one where we'll be creating a much larger and more elaborate version of The Orb as a commercial installation, one that introduces interactivity, visualization and other of our interests.

What was the process like working with such creative artists as Paul Abacus and the Early Morning Opera?

It was very open-ended. The idea was that we would come together and do an artist residency. We brought a lot of design engineering capabilities (Nick even developed some custom sound-spatializing software to make data-reactive sound with the sound artist, Nathan Ruyle), and I brought the additional aspect of having studied history as college student, and art was my degree as an undergrad.

What we were being asked to do was to create technological story-telling elements that were visualizations of a variety of different ideas. One of the big pieces was about the shift from religiosity to the green movement and understanding how to shape that argument. We had to find data to suggest that kind of stuff and design it into something for a fine art space.

It was a great way of saying, 'Hey, you're uniquely suited to do this, and you have total freedom to create a story.' What we would do was create and 'illustrate' how to tell that story with data and visuals; then the rest of the group – the writers and director involved in the project – would take that outline, write a dialogue around it and weave it into their larger narrative.

> *Innovation is life; or rather co-existence and participation. Any act, even the simplest, will inevitably cause or lead to another, even if that is silence. All is flow, says Heraclites, so to assume non-movement is to assume death.*
>
> **Rob van Kranenburg** (Author of *The Internet of Things* and co-founder of bricolabs and the founder of Council)

Not long ago I learnt that the way *2001* – the movie and the book – worked was that Arthur C Clarke and Stanley Kubrick wrote the outline together and then the book and the screenplay were created separately. It validated that process in my mind: being extremely open-ended and outlying and then finding a way to express it... outlining, based on all the things you know how to do, making that into 'something' which someone else can take and shape.

It sounds like freeform jazz, wherein there is a great base of fundamental knowledge; and, with that base you can, quite literally, play with other people to create something that could be majestic.

It really was. I felt very lucky to be a part of that.

One active process I'm engaged in is trying to figure out to what extent I can create special relationships with people as opposed to, 'I just want to hire a guy that can do xyz.'

I feel kind of like, using the jazz metaphor, I can have a tremendous, multi-dimensional relationship with other creative people when I seek out a meaningful connection through the work and, as a result, the 'music' we're going to make is going to go somewhere we never would have gone. Those are the kind of relationships that we are starting to pursue with people.

It also sounds like gardening in that, to a certain extent, the more you enrich the soil the more you can grow.

That's very, very true.

You studied at NYU, which I would imagine is a place rich with ideas and inspirational people and projects, as is New York City itself. Was there something that happened that made you realize, 'This is what I'm going to do'?

Yes. I learnt to program a computer. I had a degree in art and history and, apart from doing some calculus classes in college I didn't have any other technical experience. My father was a scientist but that wasn't my thing. I worked in theatre and a music touring company for a while; I played music for decades and decades and was in bands... all those kinds of things.

I didn't learn to program a computer for the sake of programming – that's what an eight year-old does. And I don't mean that in a bad way (and it's not always the case) but most of my engineering friends have said something along the lines of, 'Yeah, I started programming at eight or nine and I was obsessed with just getting the computer to do stuff!' I was not that kid.

But, in the early 90s, when I was playing in a lot of bands in college, I wanted to produce demos. The best way I could do that was to use some computer-based sequencing to make convincing drum tracks. So, I had to learn enough about using the computer – and this is pre-Windows – to get that one thing done. I had to learn to reset hexadecimal codes to change reverb effects. Well, actually, first I had to call and ask the guy at the software company what a hexadecimal code was. This wasn't at all what I wanted to be doing – but I did want to add reverb to make my demo better. It was always a means to an end. Later I studied art; I learnt digital art like Photoshop and other ways of creating content using a machine. I had to develop this new competency; and again, the digital part, the computer, was a means to an end.

In graduate school I learnt to design interfaces, but there, in order to create the designs and experiences I really wanted to make, I had to learn how to program. Now I program in a dozen languages, but I still see the computer, and technology, as a means to an end – a means to do something else.

I don't like to program for programming sake. I like it because of what I can do with it. I can make a data visualization, I can make a unique LED display; I can create an experience for someone to have that they wouldn't otherwise have had. Whether I do it with a circuit or programming language, with a laptop or an iPad, I don't care. It's really about what the best way of producing the 'thing' is; and that makes me a very different kind of person than those who used to work with computers in the past.

You're part of the process of IT growing into what it's supposed to be.

That's a great way of putting it.

> *The more dots you see, the more connections you make. Curiosity and the ability to discover are two key preconditions to innovation. A curious mind that has the chance to experience different ideas, cultures and perspectives will inevitably think of new things. To succeed, innovation needs to show results, albeit at a small scale. Otherwise, it's just art.*
>
> *The 'not invented here' syndrome is the main killer of innovation in large organizations, followed closely by the fear of failing. Managers who feel threatened by new approaches they have not invented will often move to quash them. The lack of accountability also hinders innovation.*

Pierre Guillaume Wielezynski (Deputy Director/ CIO at World Food Programme)

Keyword imagination exercise

Take a few minutes to close your eyes, relax and explore these keywords. You may want to make a note of any ideas that emerge that you want to explore later.

Art, Expression, Partner, Stability, Storytelling

Jeff Leitner

Jeff Leitner is the founder and Dean of Insight Labs, a foundation which brings together thought leaders to solve intractable international problems for the common good. Speaker, author and advisory board member, Jeff's former career was in public affairs, journalism and social work.

What was your 'aha moment' when you set your sights on founding Insight Labs?

Insight Labs is a peculiar combination of my assets and my liabilities. I suspect the same is true for anybody who founds anything, but I don't know that everybody is as acutely aware of it as I am. Anybody who has achieved any sort of success in what they're doing, I think they've engineered some way to stay away from the stuff they're bad at. And I think that's what this is.

It occurred to me recently why I hung out with entrepreneurs, especially technology entrepreneurs. It's because, when you're doing something audacious, something that nobody quite understands, it's nice to have other people say 'come sit with us'. Entrepreneurs, particularly technology entrepreneurs, were the folks who first said it to me. They didn't understand what I was doing but it seemed audacious and absurd, and what they were trying to do was audacious and absurd.

I think, what you've done is create a space where you can tell people, 'come sit with me'.

That's one of the things I'm good at – creating an environment in which other people believe that they're going to be able to not just sit and have a say, but that they're going to be able to think at the top of their capacities. I am able to invite the smartest people there are, and the reason I'm able to get them to stay is because they see an opportunity to work at full capacity – to think with people who are going to challenge them.

You have an illustrious alumni list of innovators and thought leaders; I imagine it is wonderfully enlivening to be surrounded by people such as these who are 'at the top of their game'. How do you determine who you want to invite to join the labs?

The same way you do.

Am I that obvious?

Yes. I ask myself: 'Who would it be a blast to think with?' How I get them to do it is a different question. Essentially, I simply say 'I want to borrow your brain.' Then I assemble a roomful of people to solve a mind-numbingly complex problem in three hours. Almost everybody says yes; the ones who don't nearly always decline because they're travelling. Nobody says it doesn't sound interesting to them.

Here's the difference between my request and your request. Your request is: 'Come share with me your wisdom so that we can help others.' I think that's a fair request. My request is: 'Come share with me your wisdom to help me solve an impossible problem and because you'll get to think something you've never thought before.'

> *Refuse to accept the notion of 'impossible'. The corners of my mouth turn up in a grin when I hear someone use that word, and I instinctively want to help them overcome that mentality.*
>
> **Jeff Power** (Strategic innovator)

How do you choose which problems you're going to look to solve?

We do it in partnership with the organizations we partner with. So, the key is partnering with the right groups from among the many who ask for our help. The three criteria we use are: 1) the leadership – which must participate – understands they face a model-related challenge; 2) the organization must have the resources and means to do something with what we develop together; and 3) the problem has to be interesting to us. We have many organizations come to us and say, 'Will you help us?' We choose only a very small handful out of those.

Speaking of interesting – I'd like to move on to innovation, which is my main area of interest right now, and the focal point of this book, after all. How do you define innovation?

It's an important question. We live in a perilous time for questions like that – not because anyone's life is threatened by the question – but because the avalanche of talk about innovation and big ideas threatens the actual value innovation might provide.

All the talk about innovation – at universities, in companies, in nearly every conceivable social gathering – numbs us to the real potential of breakthrough ideas, products and services. Consider what Facebook has done for the word 'friend'; we are seeing the same everywhere for the word 'innovation'.

Having said that... we are toying with a crazy idea that simultaneously limits and increases the value of the term. We are experimenting with the notion that innovation is, or should be, a synonym for evolution. Evolution, as Darwin laid it out for us, is a series of genetic aberrations that either better equip a species to survive or doom a species to fail. The key idea is that genetic aberrations – or innovations – aren't of value in and of themselves, but in the context of our quality of life. Does the innovation increase or decrease quality of life?

So, we define innovation, or do right now, as evolution. What's important about that, at least for us, is that it forces us to ask ourselves: sure it's new and interesting and cool, but does it advance our quality of life? Does it better equip us to survive?

> *I'm working on creating devices (cell phones, laptops, tablets) that power themselves with a small solar cell. I'm not doing this by innovating the solar cells, but by lowering the power consumption of the devices down by 10–100 times so that existing cutting-edge solar cells can power them. This will change access to information in the developing world – for the billions of people that live without steady access to power. It's also pretty interesting for the developed world where one will no longer have to worry about running out of battery.*
>
> **Mary Lou Jepsen** (CEO and founder of Pixel Qi)

Those are big questions, so what are your thoughts on the necessity of 'big government' funding to move innovation forward on a national level?

There's no real debate about whether or not we should have big government or small government in the United States. That is an optical illusion debate. In the United States, everybody wants big government – they just want it for different things. The Republican ticket, which professes to be the champions of smaller government, has called for automatic defence increases over the next five years without offering an explanation about where it's going; that is a move towards big government. In reality, if you deconstruct the party platforms, everybody wants to have an incredibly healthy amount of government spending. They just call it different things.

Now, big government or small, your other question is: what should be the role of government in funding innovation? In short, I'm wary of the idea of funding innovation as a rule, whether by government or anybody else.

I think government's role is in the support of environments. I think that's an appropriate role of government; whether it be natural environments, in which koalas can mate, or whether it's human environments in which people can live healthy and sustainable lives. Some environments are conducive to innovation and I think that's really what we're talking about.

Should government be investing directly in innovation? That's tricky, because they'd be picking winners and losers; and, in the United States, that's a free market issue; but, I'm wary of government investment in things we don't quite understand. But we do understand environments. We need good schools, good transportation, good housing and parks. I think that's how government invests wisely. I don't know about government-funded incubators. I can be persuaded, but I'm wary.

You've also mentioned that you're wary of crowdsourcing. Why is that?

Ah, that's where the snob in me comes out. I believe that not all opinions are equally valid. I come from a country that is obsessively a meritocracy. And I'm a big believer in meritocracy.

I'm a big believer that people who are better at something should rise to the top of said thing. I think that people who are smarter should get a bigger platform in the conversation. That is antithetical to 'everybody has an opinion and we should listen to everybody'.

I think some opinions are just more valid than others. I mean if you go back and use politics as an example – this probably makes it personally objectionable – when the president, whoever the president is, gives the State of the Union, people gather in offices and in cocktail parties and talk about what they thought of the speech. Everybody is entitled to an opinion, but some of them should be weighted differently. Perhaps one person has a deeper understanding of the issues at hand, another person has more inside knowledge of what the president is trying to accomplish, yet another understands the environment in which those decisions are being made.

America has always had a tension between a meritocracy and a level playing field for everybody. It is one of the most interesting things about the Great American Experiment. In the sense that we have a 200-plus-year history of electing the best and brightest and 200-plus-year history of celebrating people who don't know what they're talking about.

You formerly had a career in journalism; that must have some bearing on your perspective and in what you bring to the Insight Labs.

All three of us are former journalists. I covered government and politics, my colleagues Howell [J Malham Jr] covered arts and culture and Andrew [Benedict-Nelson] reviewed books. While I was trying to understand the Senate, Howell was following the Rolling Stones around, so he's clearly had a better career than I had.

But I'll tell you what it did for us: journalists have the ability to go into a room, in which they know nothing about what's going on and, within an hour or two, understand it well enough to explain it to everybody else. And that's kind of remarkable when you think about it. That's why we can work on healthcare and the arts and civics and philanthropy. We're really quick studies. That's the key.

 For innovation to succeed, we believe the following five guiding principles need to be followed:

Diversify your talent. *Too often, organizations staff their innovation departments primarily with 'creatives', in the belief that this type of individual will be more comfortable with and more likely to embrace the ambiguity associated with exploring new frontiers. The problem is, rarely does a more 'creative' resource actually have the know-how and/or mind-set to wrap a project and prepare it for implementation. You need 'creatives' and 'implementers' to ensure true innovation impact.*

Match customer needs with business priorities and capabilities. *Corporations and other organizations often seek innovation through technological advancements and/or the optimization of business processes. Customer- and stakeholder-driven approaches to innovation give leaders a view into other worlds, opening their minds to additional ways in which their organizations might be able to create value.*

Work within the system. *Innovation, as a term, connotes challenging the status quo. This approach can often put team members and other stakeholders on the defensive, which is unfortunate. Instead of working with you, some people can become roadblocks to innovation. We make a point of bringing everyone along with us on the journey to the development of innovation. Once individuals are bought into the premise, they are more likely to fight to make it happen.*

Define metrics of success before launch. *New-to-market products and services that take some time to return a profit may never get the opportunity to shine if measured on this metric alone. By taking a broader approach to assessing success, an organization will ultimately measure its effectiveness in creating value to the customer and to the long-term health of the organization.*

Never lose sight of your business priorities. *Priorities in a corporate or institutional environment can shift on a dime. Yet the relevance and value-added potential of innovation work is dependent on alignment with those current priorities. Investing in relationships throughout the client organization, knowing when to introduce new ideas and having adaptability are among the soft skills that any innovation team needs to have at its core.*

Brianna Sylver (Founder and president of Sylver Consulting, LLC)

Keyword imagination exercise

Capability, Crowd-source, Ideas, People, Resources

Final thoughts

As our online presence and connections increase and the 'tyranny of distance' decreases, both by orders of magnitude, individuals who authentically cultivate and nurture networks of online communities will be invaluable arbiters of an organization's true brand. Aided by innovative tools and technologies, these FWNs understand that their high touch, and highly valuable networks expect to be dealt with meaningfully, with messages that are focused purely on their personalized preferences, wants and needs.

Until recently businesses were able to get away with economic metrics as a measure of value. But with our ever more globalized society and the plethora of consumer choices available this is, in essence, an old, inward-looking accounting metric. The companies that will thrive in the highly connected and competitive GDE are those that realize that they must make a strategic shift and that ROI now stands for the customer-focused, external metric, which is return on involvement.

Me-health

Resolute and committed stakeholders at the heart of the healthcare industry

04

Access, Attention, Control, Flexibility, Legacy, Local, Roadblock, Services, Stakeholders, Solution, Wellness, 3D

The future of medicine is here. Forget about the 'Six Million Dollar Man'; no longer the trappings of TV tall tales, we have the technology not just to rebuild him but actually 3D print him... Well, perhaps not all of him – yet; but certainly large chunks of him could be manufactured to order.

Undoubtedly, the challenges in healthcare and health management are great; not least those of skyrocketing costs and a rapidly greying population. Many things we've long taken for granted such as antibiotics and vaccinations are either increasingly ineffective, outmoded, or economically unfeasible; and we simply won't be able to rely on them for much longer.

Innovation is the only key to solving the immense issues surrounding health and medicine, problems which affect every single person – be it physically, emotionally or economically, or a combination thereof. Healthcare and health management are issues that must be looked at from a global, national, regional and individual perspective – in both the public and private sector – all of which have their own challenges, responsibilities and opportunities for innovation. Medical innovations address issues such as quality of life, personal health empowerment, self-management and cost of supply. Historically, untold millions of deaths have been prevented due to innovations in medicine, and innovation will continue to save lives, now and in the future.

Many nations, out of necessity, have a history of medicinal innovation. Australia, for instance, has had a proud tradition of innovating healthcare to match the geographical barriers and vast remoteness of the continent. In 1928 the world famous Royal Flying Doctors Service began serving rural, remote and regional areas utilizing the, then, new technologies of aeroplanes and radio. Through these innovations, they were able to deliver high standards of healthcare to all Australians, regardless of where they lived. The same innovative thinking and strategic planning is needed today on a global scale, and throughout the healthcare sector.

Innovative, integrated, individual, efficient and economical are the five-star standards that any new healthcare and health management system – in particular those that are deemed to be disruptive – will be expected to meet. The status quo is no longer acceptable; gone are the days when the public was willing to acquiesce to their health matters being treated like a parcel passed around by partisan politicians, politics and policy leaders. Innovative medical research must be a priority, supported by informed policy, investment and research decisions. The range of innovation in the sector is absolutely awe inspiring – as are the dedicated men and women (and, as you will see in this chapter, some we might call girls and boys) who are leading lights in this extensive domain.

For those of us 'of a certain age', memories of 'The Six Million Dollar Man' may come to mind when bionics and bio-meds are mentioned. But these life-changing innovations are fact, not fiction, and are having an enormous effect on healthcare issues that touch wide swathes of the population, such as diabetes and epilepsy, as is additive bio-fabrication – a medical application of 3D (additive manufacturing) printing. Yes, limbs and joints are being printed and used. As are implants which, with the addition of electric conduits and a reservoir containing drugs, will be able to not only warn sufferers of an impending epileptic seizure, but also release the medicines necessary to mitigate if not prevent the seizure taking place at all.

Stupendous strides are being taken in the development of spray-on, self-healing, synthetic materials used to seal wounds; robotic surgery; and disease control such as using nanoparticles to eradicate the Hepatitis C virus. All of these programmes, however, are tied to multi-year development cycles and massive budgets.

With costs spiralling, it is interesting to note that there are innovations that take little time and money to implement. These include the test for pancreatic cancer, developed by 15-year-old Jack Andraka, which can be used multiple times and costs less than $3 per use; and the EyeNetra mobile phone add on, developed by David Schafran, which enables users to perform easy, inexpensive eye tests. The first of these innovations will undoubtedly save lives; the second will certainly change them.

Something as simple as a greater availability of eyeglasses has the potential to alter economies by enabling more people to work productively for longer. This, along with the inevitable lessening of wastage due to errors made because of poor eyesight, will surely have a positive effect on a company's, and potentially a nation's, GDP. A joint research project by the Brien Holden Vision Institute and John Hopkins University noted that an investment of US$28 billion would, in the first year, lead to a saving of US$174 billion with a follow-on annual saving of US$202 billion.

There can be no doubt that savings in healthcare must be found. These savings must be both budgetary and administrative, but they do not need to lessen the care, oversight and coverage of healthcare currently enjoyed. The Allen Consulting Group has estimated that a successful transition to e-Health in Australia would reduce health-care costs there by more than AUS$5 billion annually and have the potential to increase the nation's GDP by nearly AUS$9 billion – this with a population of 23 million people.

For nations with much larger populations, such as the UK with over 62.5 million, more than 315 million in the United States, China near-ing 1.4 billion and India close behind with 1.3 billion people, the numbers – and potential savings – are incredible. Obviously these countries support colossal consumer and care provider populations, so instead of looking for more money to fund healthcare, what is needed is redistribution of wasted funds reclaimed by innovative technology, techniques and thinking.

A resolution for redistribution is possible, but it will take a commit-ment, from all stakeholders – consumers, care givers, consultants and managers – to grasp the potential of innovative solutions to the en-demic economic problems within the industry. Innovative technology has moved much of healthcare and health management online, en-gendering the evolution of e-health. It is the potential of the resolute and responsible stakeholder that has led me to place the 'innovation of the individual' at the heart of this issue and reposition e-health as me-health.

I am not talking about personalized medications, which are designed specifically for individuals and their custom-tailored treatments – these will soon be readily available to those who can afford them. Nor am I referencing handy apps to make personal health management easier – though these innovations are valid and available. Instead, I am advocating for me-health stakeholders to demand innovative, simple, secure tools that enable them to interact with the healthcare system across geographic and health sector environs. (I specifically mention 'simple' because if a system that is cumbersome and unintuitive is brought online, its take-up will be minimal at best. One need only look at the participation numbers for Australia's Personally Controlled Electric Health Record – standing, at the time of writing, at less than 500,000 users nationwide, to see this made glaringly obvious.)

Using the internet and its related communication technologies, stakeholders can work together to improve healthcare delivery, collaboration, diagnostics and treatments, while reducing administrative duplications, errors and costs and, dare I say, ensure that easy to use, affordable, effective healthcare is available to one and all. Yes, budgetary and population pressures on the healthcare industry, at local, regional, national and global levels are rapidly increasing, as are problems of provisioning. But it is precisely in this area that innovative technologies can be of great importance and use.

The correct innovative technologies and tools can empower the healthcare sector and its stakeholders to operate as an effectively coordinated system. As such, they should enable: the integration of delivery systems and services; single points of contact, self-service and self-help; and disparate, vendor-neutral IT systems and processes to connect and coordinate with each other, and with the people who use them. Additionally, with the consolidation of medical records and services and the reduction in the duplication of healthcare efforts, wasteful expenditure should be greatly diminished and, in the long run, save millions – of dollars and lives.

Jack Andraka

Winner of the 2012 International Science Fair

Right now I'm beginning work on the Qualcomm Tricorder X Prize. The top prize of $10 million will go to the team that develops a mobile platform that accurately diagnoses 15 diseases in 30 consumers in three days. The solution also has to deliver the diagnoses via a compelling consumer experience that captures real-time information such as blood pressure, respiratory rate

Photo credit: Jane Andraka

and temperature. It has to enable consumers anywhere to assess health conditions quickly and effectively, determine if professional help is needed and answer the question, 'What do I do next?'

I'm working with a team of high school students to brainstorm and create this new technology. I'm excited to start this interesting and challenging journey with some amazing friends!

INTERVIEWS

David Schafran

David Schafran is co-founder and CEO of EyeNetra.com and an entrepreneur. With his innovative initiatives he looks to have a positive impact on the health and welfare of billions of people around the world.

Many people believe that innovators are exclusive and exclusionary, so the idea that they are open to a multidisciplinary, rather than a silo approach may surprise many people.

EyeNetra is working in healthcare in convergence with a lot of different technologies and social movements. To be an expert at any one of these things takes a lot of time and energy and that's not scalable.

It's like building an organization – if I try to do everything, as a CEO, I'd fail very quickly. So, if I want to do anything that innovative, it's the same concept: I can toil over it myself or I can incorporate other people. The challenge is how you bring people to the table in the right way. It's about recognizing people for the skills and experience they have and bringing them in, at appropriate times, for different parts of the process... Innovation doesn't happen through just one person; it's various people and various ideas from different backgrounds all fusing together into something that can actually be taken forward by the group.

It takes everyone having an open mind, being able to engage with other ideas, and contributing in ways that they may not be used to. The realm of the 'normal' workplace is not conducive to doing something 'innovative'. When creating a space for people to innovate it's important to design the process [so] folks can let down their guard and start opening up in a way they normally wouldn't do.

One way is by having a game camp for innovation. It's an amazing way to let people open up and get into a fun mind-set to co-create real solutions in real time. With an avatar for yourself your ego is not involved; it's more: 'Hey, I'm passionate about this cause so let's *do* something *now*' and less about: 'My role, my title, let's talk about doing something later…'.

EyeNetra is an extremely empowering and enabling project, and something you're obviously passionate about. What is the take-up like from the stakeholders within the healthcare system?

While doctors around the world are excited about our solution increasing access to millions of underserved, it's at the same time scary for doctors because it potentially changes their roles in significant ways. I don't envision the near future of the health IT revolution as actually replacing doctors, rather changing their roles to one of health and wellness coaches vs diagnosticians. Common tech that we aspire to be like are thermometers or pregnancy tests, except EyeNetra's device is connected to care via a mobile app.

As I understand it EyeNetra enables people to test their eyesight; it's a downloadable app that runs on a smartphone and only needs a couple of plastic lens attachments to work. Does it need an internet connection to operate?

No, it doesn't. The whole test is local and all the computational work is done on the phone, so the optical piece is actually passive. There are no 'smarts' in it whatsoever.

And the person living in a village in Bangladesh, for instance, does not need to have a smartphone? The device would come with the diagnostician.

That's the way we're developing it for the developing world. The self-test is definitely something that we see as the future but, for various reasons it makes most sense, in developing markets, for a technician to administer the test. That technician can essentially be anybody who wants to sell eyeglasses; it could be a micro entrepreneur of any sort. Maybe it's a pharmacist, maybe it's a government-run health centre, or maybe it's just a regular optical shop. Essentially what we are doing is getting people tested and connecting that demand for eye care with products and services through a cloud network.

> *I am currently working on something I call 'The Shirty Calculator'. It is a program that accurately estimates your personal UV exposure. It can also help optimize your time in the sun for optimum Vitamin D synthesis, based on your skin type. I hope it will empower people to change their habits and attitudes towards UV.*
>
> **Ethan Butson** (International science prize-winning grammar school student)

Keyword imagination exercise

Take a few minutes to close your eyes, relax and explore these keywords. You may want to make a note of any ideas that emerge that you want to explore later.

Local, Services, Solution, Stakeholders, Wellness

Gopal Chopra

Photo credit: Paul Elledge

Dr Chopra is the co-founder, President and CEO of pingmd Inc, a New York City-based healthcare solutions company, designed to reset and restore the relationship between patients and their physicians. Just prior to founding the company Dr Chopra was a senior investment banker in the healthcare group of Lazard Frères. He has practised as a neurosurgeon in Australia, India, Canada and the United States, and held faculty appointments at Stanford University and the University of Melbourne. He is associate Professor at the Fuqua School of Business, where he teaches the MBA Health Sector Management programme. Dr Chopra is the founder and host of Duke's Consumer and Wireless Healthcare conference.

As a neurosurgeon, entrepreneurial founder of innovative medical device companies, as an individual and a family man you have what could be considered to be a 360° perspective on the provisioning of healthcare.

And yet I always tell everybody that I'm just as confused as they are about getting my healthcare. My degree doesn't help me understand my insurance, my access, or what the rules are. Consuming and navigating are really big issues in healthcare.

> *Innovation can mean two things. The purest form of innovation can mean the design, creation and implementation of new ideas. But I think the innovation we see the most is the re-proposing of existing concepts into new systems. You can be a high-strung innovator who starts from zero and comes up with great new innovations, or you may be a more down-to-earth innovator, in which case you look at what you can combine to make the world better or easier.*
>
> **Dominique Guinard** (CTO and co-founder of Evrythng and WebofThings.org)

Does your medical entrepreneurship sit comfortably with your situation as a surgeon?

A lot of people go to various schools or industries and have career changes. Becoming an entrepreneur is self-evolution. I've shed the skin of a physician painfully because we're taught to think in very rigid command and control paradigms. That was a very significant change for me... to learn flexibility and humility.

Humility is not necessarily something one would imagine is rife within the surgical field.

The excuse is – and I still think this is an excuse: 'Oh, but [surgeons] are like fighter pilots. They need to think that way; they need to be trained that way, to get the best results.' I'm going to contest that. The arrogance factor really needs to be toned down because we work as a team and we deal with more than just a procedure.

Using the fighter pilot analogy: it took a multitude of people and processes, certainly with a cross-fertilization of ideas, inspirations and passions to get the plane in the air. I think that same type of analogy could fit the development of innovation in healthcare.

When you think about all the safety concerns, the greatest skill a surgeon can have is a lack of hesitation. Unfortunately we translate that into arrogance. But the key is: if I'm riding a motorbike at 100 mph, the worst thing I can do for my life is hesitate. If you look at any of the high-skill professions, hesitation is the death of the process. An entrepreneur is in exactly the same boat: don't hesitate; put your passion behind your goal.

Courage is a common thread in these interviews, wherein you know that something may not work, but you do it anyway. I would think that is also something you have to deal with as a surgeon: you know that someone might not get off the table but you still have to cut.

It's a very good analogy. If you extrapolate from hesitation to confidence: you have to be sure that this is a process that's appropriate, that you're going to get to the end of it, that you've planned ahead in your mind how you're going to achieve it, and that nothing is going to get in your way. Or, when it does, it's not going to deter you; you're going to find a way of controlling it and proceed. It's the ability to take on a roadblock and keep moving.

Do you think it matters what politician or political party is in power for the importance of, or the acknowledgment of the need for, innovation in healthcare to be accepted?

I think when you consider the impact it has on the delivery of services and the industry response, I think it does have an effect. If you stifle innovation in any way, you can't allow or implement process changes and technologies that make an impact. That kills the entrepreneurial environment, which is all about problem solving.

It's not so much the impact on healthcare, but that tools don't get built because no one can build a business around it; no one can sustain a solution, no one is supporting the implementation of anything except a large franchise solution. Unfortunately, the big companies that get the mandates have legacy systems. These codes were written 10–15 years ago. The iPhone has been around for three years, so there's a mismatch. You need to nurture an environment where you can allow innovation to penetrate, which is what this country was built on and continues to grow on.

Political engines can stifle that. I point to the regulatory agencies to the use, and direction of, funds for the implementation of digital healthcare. It's getting to the large corporations and stifling entrepreneurship. Healthcare is a conservative, regulated environment and it is the drive for better care and access options by the consumer and participants of care that will spur innovation and create a new industry to make the paradigm shift.

 Innovation is a process by which a dream turns into reality.
Ebrahim Hemmatnia (Founder and Chair of World With No Borders and founder of the WillPowered Foundation)

Keyword imagination exercise

Attention, Control, Flexibility, Legacy, Roadblock

Professor Gordon Wallace

Australian Laureate Fellow, Executive Research Director at the ARC Centre of Excellence for Electromaterials Science, and Director of the Intelligent Polymer Research Institute at the University of Wollongong, Professor Gordon Wallace (Australia/Ireland) is a multi-award-winning thought leader in the fields of electromaterials and intelligent polymers. His specialities include organic conductors, nanomaterials, additive fabrication and electrochemical probe methods of analysis, along with their use in the development of intelligent polymer systems. His focus is on the use of these tools and materials in bio-communications to improve human performance via medical bionics.

Noting how much research work you are involved in, how important is innovation in your work?

Without innovation in research we're just making incremental progress; in big areas of research, big changes in thinking are needed to solve big problems and delivering advances that have a financial return is part of that cycle. To be truly innovative we also need to be creative in how we bring people together and then how we work together as integrated teams.

You've been a fulcrum at the University of Wollongong in bringing researchers, research groups and different stakeholders together to move projects forward.

I think in research in science in particular, you're talking about long time frames. To build the research network that we have in Australia, and indeed globally, has taken 25 years. To pull those people together and keep the team together and engaged throughout the research journey has been quite an exciting challenge for us. And to see Wollongong emerge as one of the internationally recognized centres in [this] area of research has been exciting, but it's only been made possible by those connections that we have both nationally and internationally.

The importance of teamwork is consistently reflected in many of the *Innovation* interviews. I think it's also reflected in your prowess on the football [soccer] field: in that milieu you have to have your own skill set, as well as the ability to work with other players on the field to get to a particular outcome – to achieve a goal.

Absolutely. I've also been coaching soccer for the last 12 years or so, and that's one of the messages you find yourself preaching at work and on the soccer field to young people learning the trade. Particularly today in science you can be the equivalent of a Ronaldo or a Messi and feature in some short-term returns by being totally individualistic. However, if you want to make a real contribution you need to develop the individual skills that can make you a valuable member of a functional, integrated and highly effective team. Of course, part of the challenge is finding that team.

There seems to be a great lack of awareness, perhaps in particular in young people, that science and technology can indeed be 'sexy', let alone that it should be celebrated for being so vital to our lives, as individuals and to society as a whole.

We at ACES do have a fairly active outreach programme dealing with kids of all ages. We engage actively with the community at all levels because getting to parents, and getting the excitement in science and technology engendered in them, hopefully they will pass that on to the younger generation.

But I think you're right; there's a huge gap between kids in school and the excitement that's in the research laboratories. That gap has become wider and wider and we need to address that, particularly in Australia. It's just amazing that most kids don't understand the relevance of science and technology in their everyday lives.

There's a simple correlation between that and cooking, which I know I'm not the first to point out. For every young 'Master Chef' there are undoubtedly 10 kids who don't understand that food isn't 'ready-made'; that there are ingredients you have to combine to create a meal.

I like your analogy about cooking, especially when talking about younger kids. That's the fault of the people pre-packaging everything and giving it to them. The trouble with our educational system is, it's become so pre-packaged it's no wonder kids don't understand how the package got there; that's just the convenience in education, turning numbers over.

> *Currently I am working on the 'SPOONGE', a new invention to accurately deliver medicine to patients. It combines the best delivery methods of a spoon with the volumetric measuring accuracy of syringes, producing the SPOONGE. I hope it helps deliver medicine to children more accurately in the future.*
>
> **Macinley Butson** (International science prize-winning primary school student)

Perhaps it's been contrived as such so as to be convenient for the administrators of education.

We find it is becoming the same in universities and more and more in research, unfortunately. As you make research more 'quantifiable' by putting numbers on it, and the more you try to evaluate researchers, inevitably you make that education system and that research system more and more conservative. People are less likely to take risks because they won't be able to meet the numbers – the things that you tick off in boxes.

I've noticed that, over the last 10 years or so in research in Australia, the bureaucracy surrounding research has made it more conservative and more incremental. So, we're less likely to have the big innovative breakthroughs that we could have had 20 or 30 years ago.

It sounds like a culture of 'fear of failure' has been instilled into an area where it is imperative that there be no fear of failure.

Yes, and we must address that. In fact there must be failure if we want to move forward. Imagine: if you stack up a hundred different ideas and every one of them did not work the first time around, it will end up being a culmination of all those ideas, refined and integrated, that really brings the breakthroughs. So 'failure' is part of the programme to ensure progress.

> *Innovation comes in as many as eight flavours including two major types which are often referred to as 'incremental' or 'disruptive' innovation. That being said, innovation is distinctly different from invention and historically most successful innovations happen around great teams. For innovation to flourish, one needs to recognize that it is important to fail. Failure is what drives innovation and is the necessary part of the 'innovation process'. Learning, iteration, adaptation and developing models are all manifestations of failure and innovation is the ability to learn and build upon these failures.*
>
> **William Saito** (Author, technologies entrepreneur and founder/CEO at Intercur, KK)

Perhaps social media can work as an aid in giving research ideas, topics and policies a push toward moving forward; in particular as funding – both private and public – for certain research is being influenced more and more by social media, social interests, and the community at large.

Social media is an innovation which, in some ways, can make it harder for us to communicate our research. But that's not to say it's not a good idea. I think it's just a matter of catching up so that we use social media more effectively in terms of communicating ideas. It is a skill and an activity that needs resourcing alongside the research, not in place of it – even researchers only have 24 hours in a day!

Social media is all about the quick grab; so again, it comes back to that issue of pre-packaged things. Social media is really just the 'introduction' to try and get the attention of these kids. We need to be innovative about keeping them engaged because, if all they get is the introduction, we're back to that pre-packaged food idea, and they still won't understand the relevance and significance of science and technology in their lives. We have to be clever and careful about how we use social media. We have to make sure it's an integrated approach that gets their attention but then uses that attention to get the substance across.

Speaking of getting attention, I note that you have been involved in the design and innovative development of sports bras.

That was an interesting project because, like a lot of the things that we do, it's about planets lining up; not just technological planets but people planets. That project would never have arisen if a researcher hadn't visited our labs to see what we were doing with electronic textiles. Professor Julie Steele made the link back to some interesting work that she was doing on bra design and how that could be used in developing a smart bra for sports applications. And, to get another link in the planets lining up, we had people like Marks & Spencer come along and support that work.

No pun intended.

Right!

Thinking about the sports bra and noting the potential, using nanotechnology – electromaterials and intelligent polymers – to grow human skin cells, I wonder: would it be possible to combine the two techs to create a replacement for silicone implants? (I fully admit that I have some vague 'Austin Power-y imagery running through my mind when trying to picture this.) Could 'nano-tech' not just 'fix' the bra, but also fill it?

I haven't thought about it from that particular application point of view. But if you look at the generic area of medical bionics, we are trying to interface biology, or the human system, with electronics; then, we do look at both aspects. We're looking at sensors, as were incorporated into the smart bra, but we're also looking at artificial muscle technology that was incorporated into the smart bra to provide the additional support. We see them as wearable, medical bionics.

Most of our internal applications are implantable bionics which, of course, don't deal specifically with breasts or with the bra; we're talking more about sophisticated applications like nerve and muscle regeneration. But the types of materials and fabrication technologies that are being developed do enable us to transcend from wearable bionics to implantable bionics in a fairly seamless way. What we're learning, through the development and fabrication of materials for the external use of bionics, is being immediately used to advance developments in terms of implantable bionics.

We're specifically working on new materials and devices and the focus being implantable bionics at the moment, although we still have other projects in the exoskeleton/skeletal space. The real focus is on the challenges of implantable bionics, and these are going to require three-dimensional structures that have materials and biological components distributed, with control over the spatial distribution, in three dimensions. We've got biopolymers and living cells and growth factors all distributed through the structure, specifically targeted at nerve, muscle and bone regeneration, and other implants for epilepsy detection and control.

The challenge is how you integrate the materials and biological aspects and create the 3D structures. The machinery to do it is close but it's not there yet, so Australia has an opportunity to take the lead in additive bio-fabrication. There are opportunities to build the next generation of additive bio-fabrication machinery, which we can then use to build 3D structures that can be applied to solve clinical problems. This ability would also enable us to address fundamental sciences that we couldn't address before: to print out nerve and muscle cells, for instance.

Perhaps unsurprisingly, this leads me to thinking about the commercialization of research. There is certainly more focus on the commercialization of a university's intellectual property and, to a certain extent, an attempt to direct scientists and researchers to become entrepreneurs adept at selling their IP. Is that a hindrance to research or does it, in some way, assist with moving innovative thought and innovative practice forward?

I've been involved with these sorts of enterprises for decades. When they first appeared in universities, the whole idea was promoting the commercialization of science and technology. The problem was that the resources to do that properly were never made available. Most of these offices in universities developed into regulatory authorities, which are set up to minimize any risk in terms of commercialization of research coming out of the university.

> *Watson taught me something about the innovation process. It taught me that harnessing intellectual and technical diversity with a process that focuses and integrates new ideas is essential for building the complex systems of the future. My personal interests are developing in the area of architectures and methods that facilitate the creation and integration of diverse ideas in the development of complex systems like Watson.*
> **David Ferrucci** (BM Fellow, Vice President, and the principal investigator on the DeepQA (Jeopardy!-winning Watson Project)

As I see it they are not particularly set up to promote commercialization or the exploitation of knowledge. There needs to be a real change in thinking around the best way to get our knowledge out to the community; that includes the general community, industry – whoever wants the knowledge and can use it for the benefit of Australia, or whoever's funding the research. That's what we need to be concerned about, not having barriers that are set up to minimize risk; but that, unfortunately, is what's evolved.

Another barrier seems to be the current inability to share knowledge securely and 'smartly'. I am making a distinction between the current buzzwords/phrases 'big data' and 'Smart Data'; frankly, with data (and perhaps with bionic bras) size doesn't matter – it's what you do with it that counts! There are incalculable mountains of data out there, but having the ability to use that data, and disseminate it, in a simple, secure, 'Smart' way is a huge issue.

Absolutely. Exciting as all new developments in additive bio-fabrication and materials for medical devices are, what it's meant is: our ability to create 'data' has escalated exponentially. Then before disseminating that data, there's a critical step: our ability to turn that data into knowledge hasn't kept up with our ability to generate the data. So we find ourselves almost drowning in seas of information that we need to convert into knowledge.

The tools for knowledge generation are improving and yet we still seem to be stuck with so many draconian ways of communicating that knowledge. It has to be communicated at a lot of different levels, and that's a barrier because again it is not resourced and while many researchers have the skills to do it they are not supported in this area.

People often ask me: what will be the great determining factor in seeing these advances turned into clinical applications? I don't think it's technological. I think it's going to be our ability to communicate at various levels and to build effective teams. Not just teams of researchers, but having regulators and the general community involved from the start so we can take projects through, as effectively and efficiently as possible, to the enduser, which is where we want it to be.

To my mind, individuals and organizations underestimate the imperative need for collaboration to their peril – at least economically. And, with the 'flattening of the world' and the new Global Digital Economy, it is more than likely that any collaborative ecosystem, looking to become as ubiquitous as it is useful, will have to be multinational and multilingual.

I think you're right, particularly for a place like Australia. At this juncture Australia needs to be part of, and even potentially leading, some global research challenges. But we can't do that in isolation.

I took several trips around Asia last year, and the rate of progress in research and research infrastructure in those countries is absolutely staggering. I visited *one* institute of chemistry in Beijing, which has more than 900 PhD students in chemistry!

Australia needs to be engaged at a global level, and it's going to require innovative approaches to do that. This is where innovation is important, not just technologically; Australia needs to figure out ways to build effective global alliances. It's imperative if the relevance of research in Australia is to continue to be recognized.

And yet, Australia is quite a risk-averse country.

I totally agree. And all the bureaucracies and institutions that we're putting in place encourage that risk-aversion at all sorts of levels. But that's not how you do big, bold, ambitious research.

I think the bottom line is, most people think, 'We don't need to do that; we're ok for the next 5 to 10 years.' Maybe they don't even look that far ahead. But if you look beyond that, from the perspective of a scientific researcher, we need to be part of the global research community if we're going to benefit from the technological advances that will occur in the next 5 to 20 years' time. Otherwise, Australia will not have a seat in that global research community and we will suffer from it.

Australia is at the leading edge of areas such as additive bio-fabrication, and we have the opportunity to stay there. But we have to take a few risks in an environment that encourages us to do so. We have to get out there and be bold and ambitious with our research vision and execute dynamic, appropriately resourced research programmes.

> *In my own experience discretionary funding is not a luxury but an imperative. Discretionary funding – money beyond what it takes to meet an organization's basic obligations and expectations – is the most important catalyst to innovation. It means that one can have the freedom to 'fool around' – to try and fail – and still support one's family. Money is time as well as freedom in the sense that it buys the time and legitimacy to innovate.*

The greatest barrier for innovation is our innate conservatism. And by that I mean an adaptive human trait of adhering to what we know and trust for longer than we probably should, resisting innovation and therefore communicating ambivalence about innovators. We applaud them once their innovation receives wide praise but we recoil at initial stages, fearing that their 'innovative' idea may be sheer madness. In my experience true innovators are a bit 'deviant'. I mean that literally: they deviate from what society anoints as 'the norm'. Leaders who understand the imperative of innovation not only encourage employees to innovate, they protect them, and also set aside funds to enable employees with the insight, perspicacity and courage to innovate.

Abby Bloom (Co-founder and CEO of Acu Rate and thought leader in innovation in healthcare and medical devices)

Keyword imagination exercise

Commercialization, Effective, Fear, International, Team

Final thoughts

Innovation, in one form or another, and depending upon the tools and technologies available at the time, has always been a part of healthcare and health management. Currently we are witnessing tremendous breakthroughs that empower people to manage their own health more effectively, as well as those that extend and improve our longevity and the quality of life for our rapidly aging society. All that said, it may be that a more efficient administrative system will have the greatest effect on healthcare. As with the effective use of innovative tools and technologies, budgets will not need to be cut but instead can be redistributed – and in doing so save time, money and lives.

Innovating educating

05

Breadth,
Commitment, Community,
Cost, Cross-discipline, Depth,
Environment, Experience, Global, Goals,
Message, Open, Profit, Resolution, Silo, Wealth

I'm exceedingly happy to grab an opportunity to quote Pink Floyd's 'Another Brick in the Wall Part 2': 'We don't need no education...', but in the 21st century the message is totally wrong. What we don't need is the *same* education. And as for 'thought control', due to innovative technologies and tools those being educated are more likely to be controlling the thoughts being taught – the lessons – than ever before. Everywhere you look, education and the systems that surround and support it are changing. Around the world more people are accessing more education, particularly online. This will have a lasting effect on their lives and livelihoods as well as affecting economies at a local, national and supranational level. It will certainly change the industry of education as we know it.

As the Majority World takes up the online education available to them, there is little need for them to incur the expense of national or international travel to gain access to texts and teachers that were formerly out of reach. However, it must be noted that there are many national budgets that currently rely on the influx of, and income from, foreign students. When that income dips, as nations such as the UK and Australia can readily attest to, it bites the budget. Simply put, having fewer foreign students affects a nation's GDP in the GDE. As the infrastructure and availability of accredited courses increase, home schooling may become the norm throughout the world.

As of yet, there are still improvements needed in online education before it can be given an A grade. For instance, accessing online education must be simple, secure and inexpensive – which means that access to the internet and mobile data must be affordable. Additionally, innovative tools must be developed that do not depend on high speed broadband access, which is unlikely to be available to the bulk of the majority world for some time. If they are to be ubiquitously used, these tools must empower and enable seamless cooperation and collaboration, therefore they must be multilingual in nature.

Just as empowered endusers will expect individually tailored marketing and advertising campaigns that answer their particular wants and needs, it is likely that these same expectations will apply in the world of online education. Online educational programmes will be expected to differentiate themselves in terms of content, price, brand and accreditation availability – something that, currently, eludes the industry. Innovations in the sector will mean that 'one size will *not* fit all', as online students will soon expect to study a curriculum in a style that has been distinctly designed either for, or by, them.

One can only wonder at what is on the cards for teachers. Will they be expected to be entertainers that are accessible to their students anywhere at any time? Historically, teachers have spent huge numbers of hours with their charges and as such they've been in a position to be particularly influential. Who will take up this mission when students no longer attend classes but merely log on? Will online teachers still have the same responsibility to lead? Will their classes become Facebook pages or Twitter trends?

The answers to these questions may change quickly as more technology and tools come to the fore. What will not alter is the need for those in STEM (Science, Technology, Engineering and Maths) to embrace the evolution to STEAM – with the addition of Art to the mix – and acknowledge culture as an imperative to collaborative innovation. It is with the cross-fertilization – the mixing and mingling if you will – of all of these topics, which leads to innovative thought, processes and products. Steve Jobs and his work with Apple, Pixar, etc, was a great example of this embodied in one man.

The collaboration and cooperation between universities and business is also of great importance to the success of innovation. Aligning what's being taught and researched in universities with what business actually wants and needs can only assist in the development of innovative tools. Frankly, it doesn't matter how brilliant a technology is, if no one uses it there is no point having a superb solution to a problem that doesn't exit.

There is no better way to ponder what problems need solving than to discuss the subject with the intended enduser. Better yet, why not include the enduser in the process? As universities look for ever more necessary funds by capitalizing on their intellectual property, it makes sense that they develop 'products' that people actually want to purchase. In doing so, they may be able to maintain the ivory towers of pure research that they are used to being able to afford.

As educators may be expected to become more entertaining, so too scientists may need to add salesmanship to their list of core skills as R&D evolves into RD&C (Research, Development and Commercialization). Universities are already in the midst of major changes as they move from being institutions of unlimited learning potential towards being places of unlimited earning potential.

According to the (US) President's Council of Economic Advisers, nearly US$4 trillion is spent globally on education each year. This is nearly 6 percent of the world's GDP. With numbers like that, it comes as no surprise that there is a battle brewing between those who see education as a lucrative for-profit business and those who view it as a non-profit human right.

It is estimated that there are now 7 million people studying online. The advent of MOOCs (Massive Open Online Courses) has gone a long way to extend education beyond the, what some might term, elite group that can afford to attend campus-based colleges and universities. MOOCs equate to easily accessible education available via such notable initiatives as the Khan Academy, Udacity and Coursera. Top-notch – and top dollar – universities such as MIT, Stanford, Berkley, Harvard and Yale have joined the fray by putting various courses and course material online via iTunes, YouTube and other web-based media. What is not yet on offer is full-blooded accreditation rather than some semblance of an 'acknowledgement of accomplishment' certificate. This leads to the question: how much 'cred' should 'tread' be worth, ie how much more valuable is an education gained from physically attending classes than its virtual counterpart – and how long will this difference remain?

'Fee or free?' can be a divisive question. Just look at how polarizing and politically charged open knowledge can be, as evidenced by the attempted prosecution, and eventual suicide, of Aaron Swartz, co-founder of the online free content provider, Reddit. Charged with stealing millions of archived scientific journals from MIT with a view to making them freely available, Swartz was seen by some as a hero of the open source, open information movement while others saw him as intentionally ruining the economic value of information. This, as the United Kingdom and the European Commission are spearheading the call to make tax-funded academic research available for free and Harvard is encouraging its faculty to make their research available via open access journals and avoid academic publishers that keep articles behind paywalls.

Institutions could save millions of dollars a year if the requirement to pay for access to academic research is removed – these savings could, potentially, fund scholarships and further research. But one must ask, where does the balance lie between intellectual property rights and the right to a proper education? What is certain is that new business models will be required for educational establishments and the industries such as academic publishers that surround them.

INTERVIEWS

Adam Glick

Adam Glick is president of the Jack Parker Corporation and a managing director at the hedge fund Tesuji Partners. An author and playwright, Mr Glick is the President and co-founder of the Floating University.

What compelled you to start the Floating University?

There were two 'aha moments'. The first was in business: I was having great difficulty hiring people with perspective. There are very, very smart people who are very, very talented within the silo of whatever discipline they have come through, be it in college or in earlier jobs. But they lacked the 'putting-it-all-together-now' skill. At the time, I was thinking: why is this occurring?

The coincidence was that my son was looking around at colleges. The first college was identical to the second college, which was identical to the third. I thought: why aren't there courses in colleges, especially early on, that are 'an inch deep and a mile wide'; and why aren't there cross-disciplinary courses? Of course, the reason is because it's harder for a school to do. The school sets up, for the faculty, into silos of different majors.

They can't offer a course like the 'Great Big Ideas' course that we're currently offering at the Floating University, because it involves somebody from physics, somebody from political philosophy, somebody from psychology, somebody from classics departments, and so on... the politics of putting together a course like that are virtually impossible. But, on the internet, you can film the best physicists, the best psychologists, sociologists and biologists and provide some sort of connection in the classroom. It flips the whole experience around. Instead of going to class for a lecture then going home to your dorm room and having interesting discussions about it, we have the lecture at home – on the internet – and have the dorm room work as the class.

I think the biggest imperative for innovation is the willingness to take risk. If you want to make a big impact, you have to take a big risk – there's simply no way around it. The people (or countries or regions) that can understand that tend to be the most innovative. For example, Israel lives with an existential risk – this makes their people much more risk-tolerant than, say, Europe. I often see countries or regions implementing an 'innovation ecosystem' without the corollary of accepting risk in new ventures. Many people are interested in innovation without accepting the corresponding risk of failure that goes along with that.

That brings me to the greatest barrier I see, which is probably the cultural acceptance of risk and, more important, failure. If I set up a company in Europe and it fails, then I'm considered a failure. The same failure in Silicon Valley is called Experience (with a capital E!). A very visible manifestation of this is regulatory. A hidden secret of the success of entrepreneurship in the US is that if your company fails, it's relatively easy to shut it down. In Spain or Italy if that happens, first criminal charges are laid and then they ask what happened. I set up a subsidiary in India once for one of my companies and when the company failed, I tried to shut it down. It took me seven years. Am I likely to do another company in India? Extremely unlikely. Countries and regions that want to embrace innovation also have to make it easy to fail and shift the cultural bias against that.

Salim Ismail (Co-founder, Executive Director and Global Ambassador for the Singularity University and Chairman of Confabb)

I'm a fan of a good, liberal arts, broad-based education and the non-siloing of experience. Taking the motto of the Floating University: 'Through breadth to depth' – what does that breadth and depth bring to you, as an employer?

I think there're two things about the breadth that are important before we can get to the employer thing.

The first thing is that I don't get the notion that the purpose of an undergraduate education is to get you a better job. I think that it used to be to make you more broad so you could enjoy the world more. I think you should go to college to learn how to enjoy the world and to learn how to improve your world. We've completely focused on the 'improve' and we've dropped the 'enjoy' entirely. Part of the ethos of the Floating University, is to get students to really hold a mirror up to themselves. The next step is that people who are self-aware tend to be better in business.

Noting how expensive attending colleges and universities can be, do you think that the Floating University and its ilk are the future of higher education?

We're at a very early stage – not even the first innings – as to the evolution of education, but I will give you two models. The simplest is this: introductory economics in the United States is taught 15,000 times every fall and every spring. Now, there has to be one guy who is the best at teaching that. Imagine if we filmed him and gave him to the 14,999 schools that he's not currently teaching at. The second thing is: in the United States, at least, the cost of higher education has increased, for the last four years, at twice that of inflation.

At first that sounds completely crappy. If you think about it for a moment, all business has to achieve productivity gains; but in education the only way to achieve quality gains is through productivity losses. Instead of one person teaching 30 people, one person now teaches 15. I think that the internet will completely change that.

I don't think it will change it at the very top – at the Harvard, Yale and Princetons of the world – because their credentials will be worth so much. But just go one rung below and I think there will be massive changes. That said, I still think there will be some value for a residential education. There is a lot that can happen in the dining hall and dorm room.

It might also lead to the equivalent of a space race in education. I can imagine thousands of introductory economics professors wanting the kudos of being 'number one' and part of the Floating University, or its equivalent. There's a potential for raising the level of teaching altogether.

There's a yes and no to this. The analogy that I give is Hollywood. It used to be that actors were tied to a studio. That's the model that academics work in now; teachers are tied to a school. Why should the teacher be tied to a school in the future? They won't be. They will float and they will give a lecture here, or they'll give lectures for my business or somebody else's business, etc.

> *I am working on enhancing the efficiency of massive, open, online education by combining it with the untapped potential of virtual reality for the creation of virtual communities of practice. Based on the psychological power of the avatar I hope to bring back the 'wow' factor and help trainers and organizations design, develop and facilitate passion-driven, enthusiastic and enjoyable learning experiences.*
> **Stylianos Mystakidis** (Award-winning designer, developer and facilitator of e-learning and virtual immersive environments)

So should education be a business?

Totally good question. I don't know the answer, but I do believe that there should be a model. There's a million different models for education so I think that it can be offered for free, it can be offered as a business, as a not-for-profit, et cetera, et cetera.

You mentioned that the evolution of education isn't even in its first innings. Where do you see the Floating University being at the bottom of the ninth?

My basic business philosophy is ready, fire, aim. So I haven't a clue.

In general, it's so easy to spend so much time painting the can that you never get off it. I think people overestimate the difficulty of changing mistakes.

The first video we did for the Floating University... we thought it should be filmed live, so we had the whole thing set up. We had a big audience, etc; it was big. Everything was wrong about it. We stopped. We lost three months. We went back. We rethought the whole thing. I think, in most businesses, there are very few mistakes you can't fix some way, somehow.

People can spend a great deal more time making a business plan than they do making the business.

Exactly. We have never written a business plan, there's no mission statement, we don't have a clue. You have to be able to improvise and improvise and improvise.

And tap dance if you can.

Exactly.

> *I am working on something [the Move India Foundation] that will change India and maybe the world... in my spare time. The problem of school dropouts in India is incredibly high. Estimates are that three out of four children drop out of school, leading to over 300 million people in India having no education or vocational skills. There are many noble efforts focusing on literacy but I am focusing my efforts on vocational skilling for these dropouts.*

A social experiment that I conducted over the last four years showed that one could increase earning capacity for a school dropout by a factor of five by giving them a single skill, such as a course in motorcycle maintenance; such a young person could now lead a normal life. The question is how you do this for 300 million young people.

I have created the non-profit Move India Foundation, which has a vision of training 1 million school dropouts per year. Our key learning so far: given that we are talking about millions of people, widely distributed, we need to take training to the people rather than bring people to the training. Our innovation is to create specialized buses – such as a carpentry bus, a plumbing bus, a tailoring bus, etc – where each bus is a mobile vocational classroom.

The buses will be fully equipped with seats, projection equipment, learning tablets, workbenches and tools. They will travel with one or more instructors and visit villages on a fixed schedule. The buses will be equipped with content for a particular skill, connected to the internet, made available in an open-source format, with flexibility in language selection, local adaptation and refinement. In strong alignment with the

Government of India's programme of modular, employable skills, these buses will be operated by vocational training organizations to expand their reach into the hinterland of India, where millions of young people are eager to gain new skills and opportunities. In about one month new carpenters, plumbers and tailors can be created using this model.

If we succeed, we will have changed India in a dramatic way. Villagers need not travel to the cities in search of education and employment. When practical vocational training is available in the village, new entrepreneurs are created. These entrepreneurs will set up shop locally, servicing the needs of the community. That increases the economic base, reducing migration to cities. Specializations start to develop and economically viable local communities are created. It is still at an early stage, but we are making progress in creating the prototype.

Sridhar Jagannathan (Founder of the Move India Foundation and Chief Innovation Officer at Persistent Systems)

Keyword imagination exercise

Take a few minutes to close your eyes, relax and explore these keywords. You may want to make a note of any ideas that emerge that you want to explore later.

Cross-discipline, Depth, Experience, Profit, Silo

Bill Liao

Internationally renowned entrepreneur, philanthropist, diplomat, speaker and author Bill Liao is a venture partner with SOSventures, co-founder of the social network service XING and founder of the non-profit organization WeForest.com and co-founder of CoderDojo.

One of the reasons that I began writing this book is that I became aware that not all innovators are able to tell their story well. You certainly do not have that problem.

You know, people think of sergeants as the guys who just yell at you. But actually, most sergeants take the incomprehensible orders of their commanders and turn them into a short narrative that allows you to fully grasp what is needed at the time and buy into it.

While you are exceedingly comprehensible and renowned for nuanced narrative yourself, you've brought in the brilliant wordsmith and modern day minstrel, Stephen Fry, to tell the tale of WeForest and its mission of reforestation to counter global warming – an issue which, undoubtedly, needs to be grasped and bought into.

Absolutely; we gave him a brilliant story to tell. Without a crisis, a struggle and a resolution in the story, nobody's going to listen. So you've got to have a great storyteller and you've got to have a great story.

You can have a fantastic innovation, but unless you tell a good story about it, it's never going to get anywhere. The start of the traction for innovation is being able to communicate it succinctly in an emotionally engaging way.

> *While helping celebrities and global brands over the past few years build their social media presence, I recognized a need for dedicated social media education. In 2011, I launched a new division of my company, Digital Royalty University to help educate corporate brands, personalities, celebrities and athletes on the power of social media. More recently, we expanded to include all individuals, not just companies and brands, and our classes are now available online. We believe that social media can be a force for good in the world, which is why we partnered with Teach For America to be the recipient of our Buy One, Give One Programme. For every Digital Royalty University class purchased, a class will be given to a teacher, helping to close the communication gap between parents and teachers in low-income schools. Studies show that students achieve more when their parents are involved.*
>
> **Amy Jo Martin** (Founder and CEO of Digital Royalty)

You're illustrating your commitment to the future of the planet with WeForest. One might posit that your work with CoderDojo, and its work to teach children to code, is also a commitment to the future. Why do you feel it is important that children learn to be creators rather than just users of technology?

Because human beings are remarkably programmable and a lot of people are figuring that out. And as far as I'm concerned, in our future you're either going to program or be programmed. Plus, the more creators you have in the computer industry the better, simply because the scarcest resource on earth today is not oil; it is talented programmers and developers who play well with others. The growth in our application technology is double-digit exponential. The growth in our development of human beings who can service that, in the innovation industry, is not.

You seem to have a healthy balance of pragmatism, possibility and potential. So, are you hopeful for the future?

I'm not a great fan of hope. There is a great book, *Hope is Not a Strategy* by Rick Page; everything about that is self-evidenced. I am resolutely optimistic, while at the same time greatly pragmatic. And that's the balance.

It takes a certain degree of mental discipline to hold two very polarizing thoughts in your mind and continue to operate. In a way, innovation is directly related to that ability. If you're an optimist and a pragmatist, and you can hold those two thoughts and feelings in your head at once, then that illuminates a certain path, given at least a reasonable background knowledge of what the problem is.

I get irritated by people who are just happy-clappy. Richard Wiseman did a fantastic study which he put in his book, *59 Seconds*, that shows that people who visualize attaining their goals are actually less likely to achieve them.

Is that because they're visualizing goals rather than attaining them?

They visualize the attainment of the goal, have a big rush of endorphins and go: 'Wow, I'm pretty cool!', and actually do nothing. Whereas people who visualize the hard effort of the pathway that goes towards the goal are more likely to achieve them. So the 'happy-clappy, it's all good, just allow the universe to take care of it' brigade drives me nuts.

At the same time I also have very little time for pessimists. I'm a great believer in self-development itself. I believe that you can innovate your own personality as much as you can innovate externally. But, to do it just for the sake of doing it, without getting any traction – that's just a waste of everyone's time.

> *It's essential that innovation be built on a foundation of solving a problem or helping people reach a goal. Too many meetings are engineered where marketing people get really excited about an idea or feature but, in the end, if it doesn't do anything to solve a problem or reach a goal it never gets any traction in the marketplace. However, I've become deeply convicted that even if it does those things, if it's not communicated effectively it never gains any ground.*
> **Keith Ogorek** (SVP and Marketing Director at Author Solutions)

Keyword imagination exercise

Commitment, Global, Goals, Message, Resolution

Lizbeth Goodman

Lizbeth Goodman is Professor of Inclusive Design and Chair of Creative Technology Innovation at University College Dublin and board member at the Innovation Academy. Founder and Director of SMARTlab, Director of Research at Futurelab Education, Lizbeth has won numerous international accolades including the Blackberry Outstanding Woman in Technology and the Microsoft Innovation in Education Award. She is a sought-after researcher, writer, presenter, performer, and thought leader in a wide range of fields including arts/media programming and body language engineering interfaces for rehabilitation.

What a career you've had – you seem to embody the clarion call for innovators to have a breadth and depth of experience. What was the impetus for the direction you took?

Like most careers in any field, some of it was serendipity – being at the right place at the right time or the wrong place at the right time. Sometimes branches lead to unexpected places. But, because I had very, very poor vision as a child I've always been hugely aware that, without innovative technologies, including contact lenses – really high-powered ones, which are the only reason I can function in the world – all but the wealthy simply wouldn't be able to contribute much to creating a more equal society.

My first job, at the age of 2... was tapping toes in America. It was a little TV act, and that was my college fund. College is very expensive in the States so my parents put us on TV to save for college. But I wouldn't have been able to do that without the advances in technology that allowed me to see and, therefore, move freely. I feel so grateful that I lived at a moment in time, and in a part of the world, where these things were possible, even for families who didn't have a lot of money. I think that's been a framing context for the way I, metaphorically, see the world and probably explains why I'm interested in the kind of projects I do.

There have been a few really defining moments: like the first job I had at the Open University, which was on the BBC. My very first lecture turned out to be for 6 million people! Straight out of graduate school and right into the fire, because all of our lectures were televised on BBC 2. At that time there were only four channels, so millions of people would tune in to watch. You had to, somehow, engage the audience because viewing figures counted.

I had a lot of media training so it didn't bother me at the time, and it became a great opportunity. There might have been 6,000 registered students, which is quite enough to have to think about in terms of a group of people with a specific learning or communication objective, let alone the millions of [non-registered student] viewers who you just had to keep interested.

It really got me thinking. Technology had to do several important things at the time and none of the technologies available could do any of those things. It was, basically, mandatory to invent a whole new system, which is what we did. We set up a team at the BBC making truly effective, interactive teaching and communicatory tools and, 20-odd years later, that team is still behind SMARTlab.

Every now and then we'll form a new research group because there will be some social needs that a whole community, country or culture has. Perhaps it's one individual that has a need that won't be addressed by anything that exists and which no government, health service or education system is going to fund.

For all the lip service that everyone pays to accessibility, disability, women's safety and the rest, it just isn't the case – at least not anywhere that I've ever been – that everyone is served at the level they need to be. So, now and then, we reboot ourselves when we realize that, despite everything, there's still somebody, somewhere, who can't communicate, or can't realize their full potential, unless we dig in and start again intellectually and, in terms of technology, innovate to create something completely different. Every couple of years we meet one of those pivotal people, or one of those extreme user groups, and we form a new research group to address those new problems.

We have the evidence that labs like ours can, and do, change lives. The Club Tech project with Microsoft has now reached 7 million people. Other projects might reach only one person, but so long as that contact leads to something transformative, I think the ripple effect from these can be huge.

> *Both my father's lifetime work at* The Economist *and my idea of a career as a 21-year-old were totally changed in 1972 when we first saw 500 youths sharing knowledge around an early digital network. Through our different peer networks we spent the next decade debating how the first internet generation could participate in the greatest changes in human history ever staged. We branded leadership debates of this sort 'Entrepreneurial revolution'. A study of the world's most innovative people concluded that, in the pre-networked world, the average person spent less than 0.1 percent of their life at the experiential edge of their own most unique competence. Imagine [the innovation possible] in a world where we raised that by an order of magnitude.*
> **Christopher Macrae** (Author and multi-award-winning global thought leader in the fields of sustainable investment and economics)

You are extremely well respected within the innovation community, which seems to be very male-dominated. How do you think we could bring more girls and women into the innovation fold?

I think so much of it is publicizing the good work that so many women do. As always, part of the problem is that the old boys' network refuses to acknowledge, validate and publish women's work, as well as the usual glass ceiling effect wherein guys rise to the top and hire their younger role models.

The way to combat it is to keep demonstrating excellent female role models and to keep bringing to attention all the women around the world who, in so many cultures and so many languages other than English, are doing such inspiring work.

Your work with Futurelab Education illustrates your commitment to innovation in education. Why is this issue so important to you?

Because education is the foundation for human communication and for individual and community growth; yet it is entirely broken worldwide. I've come to the conclusion that the systems of education cannot be fixed by a new policy here or a bit of Blu-Tack or staple over there, which is the way that policy makers internationally are trying to fix things.

Economically, it's expensive to start again, but education needs a total reboot. It needs a different value system that recognizes not only multiple intelligences but also emotional intelligences, social intelligences, courtesy, collaboration and competition, and incorporates the kind of buddy system whereby people who learn differently are in the same classroom.

It needs different buildings with windows that are lower so that little children and people in wheelchairs can see out. It needs wireless... it just needs everything to change: the assessment system, the curriculum, the attitudes, the assumption that you need to break everybody's thinking down into 20- or 40-minute time blocks. All these things that were important, for reasons of organizational simplicity, are now blocking the development of the human race.

What difference do you think that an empowered enduser could have on society?

Absolutely transformational! There are so many people, all over the world, of different ages and at different levels of intellectual 'so-called' ability – by standard scales – in all kinds of cultures.

The only way to empower, channel and use those intelligences and talents is to provide them with accessible tools. Whether it is contact lenses for blind people like me or voice boxes for people who can't speak.... It doesn't matter what the technology is – unless we're including the whole world's population we're losing enormous amounts of the world's intelligence. That's why we're falling behind.

And it's about accessibility. If you have to remember passwords or it is necessary to be able to hold your hands very still to hit a button, then most of the elderly community won't be able to use our tools. Then we lose the wisdom of the elders – all the things they know, through life experience, are suddenly lost to the new generation. It is about creating accessible, easy to use, stable, sometimes big and clunky interfaces that the elderly and people with communication difficulties can use as easily as everyone else.

It cannot be about a profit margin, which is where the whole open source input has come in. Industries have to survive, of course; there will always be specific apps that they will sell to make their money. But, if every industry is creating the same things, just making them look slicker and slicker to compete with each other, there's so much wasted time, effort, energy and materials, and so little impact on innovation.

Innovation has got to be about learning more, faster; and to learn more, faster, as a human race we need to get more people into the conversation.

> *Any product, process or idea that helps to reduce the workload of mankind and helps to make life easier can be defined as innovation. Man (sic), in general, is a lazy animal who is always on the lookout for an easier way to do things. It is this latent characteristic of laziness that has prompted some of the greatest innovations known in today's world, right from the wheel to the smartphone.*
>
> **Nitten Nair** (Digital and social media strategist)

Keyword imagination exercise

Culture, Empower, Engage, Validate, Wealth

Final thoughts

The speed at which the industry of education is changing, with the advent of innovative technologies and tools, is astonishing. And with that change come great opportunities such as online access to information that was once kept in the 'ivory towers' of academia. However, with this augmented access comes increased competition for staff, students and ratings – both for the educational value of courses and those that lead them.

While the ability to think creatively and be open to innovation is an increasingly sought-after skill, most innovators will admit that this was a trait that, either intentionally or inadvertently, was nearly extinguished rather than enhanced during their years in education. Generally this is not the fault of the educator but simply the result of a system steeped in archaic traditions and which is essentially risk-averse and addicted to metrics that are self-fulfilling and inward looking.

It is incumbent upon all parties within academia to acknowledge that the system is in need of repair and readjustment. So that academia can maintain its relevance it needs to arm students with the tools to create a better standard of living for themselves, their families, communities and society as a whole and, perhaps of equal importance, to bolster their backbones so that they are resolute in facing risk and do not falter if they meet failure along their way.

The power of the me-dia

06

Demanding what you want delivered when, where and how you want it

Alliance, Connect, Consumer, Creative, Deliver, Demand, Do, Enduser, Evolve, Feedback, Influence, Information, Interact, Online, Permission, Public, Publish, Share, Social, Tribe, Viral

The innovation, influence and empowerment of bloggers and micro-bloggers in the new me-dia space – be it social or otherwise – has created a colossal displacement of power both politically, as discussed in earlier chapters, and commercially. Perhaps this shift, which is as deep as it is wide, is seen nowhere more so than in the media.

Oscar Wilde, in his familiar fine form noted, 'The only thing worse than being talked about is not being talked about.' I don't know if he'd be of the same opinion in the era of social media, incessant popup ads, 24/7 news channels and chatter, Twitter postings and other media outlets.

With a media where individuals are at the heart of the subject matter, rather than it mattering what is at the heart of the subject, there is an understandable semblance of schizophrenia surrounding the term 'viral': it's great if your 'good news' spreads rapidly around the world, but woe-betide those whose bad news escapes the confines of their 'firewall' and runs amok through the numerous networks that proliferate online.

The power of the network has changed very much in favour of the empowered enduser/consumer. The demand is for 'the message' to be focused, via bona fide micro-targeting, and nuanced to cater to an individual enduser's particular wants. It may be that these demands have forever changed conventional media into the individual-centric 'me-dia' it is today, which is in direct juxtaposition to the traditional formats focused on large market segments.

It is increasingly necessary for businesses that are part and parcel of what is considered traditional media to bring innovation and innovative thinking to bear. Without doubt, long-established business models are gone for all but the most stubborn – and, some would say, foolhardy. The book industry is in upheaval. Publishers, historically, have the job of putting books on shelves. But, as is the case with e-books (and, now, enhanced e-books and online ecosystems – as evidenced by the accompanying, first of its kind, publishing format of !nnovation), the question is: what is a publisher's job if there are no bookshelves to stock? How will publishers reinvent themselves? It is incumbent upon the publishing industry to find new ways to be relevant, perhaps by finding ways for readers to browse virtual bookshelves in ways that are as evocative as visiting a favourite book store used to be. Solutions to these issues will entail innovative tools that empower readers.

I am working on a cook book at the moment that will hopefully contain QR codes and other forms of interactive videos. Also, page reading technology will hopefully be included in the book, but like everything it will all come down to cost.

Tom Kerridge, internationally-renowned Michelin-starred chef

Certainly would-be authors have innovative technology at their fingertips, which empowers them to publish e-books on a whim; for some, this has led to unmitigated success. If authors are 'doing it for themselves', what happens to those professions and professionals once wrapped up in the publishing parcel of proofreading, editing, layout, etc? Many have changed from in-house to freelance. Whereas, prior to the e-book exodus authors had many a hoop to jump through before being able to get near the inner circle of editors, etc, now they need only do an online search for talent and, quite literally, millions of results are at their foraging fingertips. There are also copious companies online that have been established to enable and empower writers with free, near-free, or fee-structured services.

'Fee or free' is a conundrum – some might say a cancer – that is eating away at the business models of traditional news outlets such as newspapers, magazines and news networks. Very few 'ink and paper' newspapers have been successful in finding a charge-for-access online model that hasn't lost them both revenue and readers. The UK's *Guardian* and *Financial Times* newspapers may be two of the few that have done so successfully, but for every success story there are many media failures left lost and floundering, if not completely flopped.

One of the consequences of this has been a consolidation of companies: Viacom, Time Warner and News Corp immediately come to mind. Has the fact that so much media are now concentrated in so few hands had an adverse effect on the quality made available? Has new-media made traditional journalism passé or, perhaps, further 'dumbed down' the dailies? Is it wrong that many people now look to a self-confessed comedian, Jon Stewart, for insight and investigation on Comedy Central's 'The Daily Show'? Do we have a right to demand more from those who profess to be professionals?

There are certainly demands for greater transparency in the media, not least in declaring vested interests involved in setting precedent and agendas. It is not a great leap to believe that mass media, held in so few hands, might lead to censorship and partisanship either directly or indirectly. Of course bloggers and micro-bloggers are often partisan but, generally, they are not paid to be – or assumed to be – impartial. Conversely, those who call themselves journalists should be expected to bring judicious analysis – and yes, dare I say it, balanced reporting – along with a breadth and depth of knowledge and experience to their news stories.

So where is the innovation in this, you may ask? Innovative technology is cresting the horizon, which will empower readers to 'have it all'; and an innovative approach to adapting business and funding models will enable interested stakeholders to remain in business. Crowd-funding is already being used as a vehicle to finance science, social initiatives, art projects, magazines and books. It could also be used to fund freedom – from the current shackles of push advertising, which is increasingly falling on deaf ears. Technology is arriving that will enable innovative revenue models that are applicable not only to magazines, newspapers and other media, but also to a myriad of businesses that currently rely on push advertising for revenue.

As media increasingly becomes me-dia, readers, viewers – the endusers – could find themselves in the powerful position of being able to direct that change. With the plethora of avenues available to get their news 'fix', readers taking what they want rather than what they're given is the name of this new game. That said, an off button may remain the most powerful tool an enduser will ever have.

INTERVIEWS

David Bohrman

President of Current TV, David Bohrman has an extensive career spanning more than three decades. As a television and new media executive he has worked in network, cable, new and online media, collecting numerous awards including Emmy, Peabody and Press Club awards. He is a globally respected thought leader who has been at the helm of some of the most innovative and impactful changes in news programming and special event news coverage.

You've been 'figuring out how to do things better' throughout your career. Can you tell me more about what you call 'tinkering'?

Here's an early example: in 1987, I was part of ABC News, largely in a special events senior producer role, getting ready for the 1988 Presidential election campaign. For 30–40 years, producers had given anchors information about political conventions, candidates and speeches on 5 x 8 cards, which was antiquated and sort of dumb. We were in the computer era... although the ABC computer system was non-existent.

I stumbled across HyperCard as it was debuting. I made a demo for the guy I worked for – so, instead of having a pile of cards, you could push a button and get bios and information. He said, 'You won't pull it off but go ahead and try.' I contacted Apple and we ended up creating what was then called a HyperCard stack. If you saw it today, you would call it a website.

I did a major chunk of the programming and a guy from Apple did some of the harder parts. Peter Jennings used it on the air throughout the entire election year and it then led to the creation of ABC news interactive, which was the first new media unit at any network. It was just triggered by me wanting to figure out a better way to do the job that we needed to do: covering and getting information for elections and conventions. This won the top award in Apple/Macworld's first SuperStacks competition and the best custom HyperCard Stack.

The fact that my undergraduate education started in physics and astronomy gave me some background that's different from most television producers. I could deal with the computer stuff and I knew what was going to be able to happen, eventually.

Actually, I write very few memos – I must have written five in my 13 years in ABC – but there's one I wrote called 'the future' where I laid out, in 1990, what I thought was going to happen. It was really accurate. It was three years before the world wide web and included everything we do today, from video-on-demand to live streaming... and it was laughed off by a very new management group that had just bought ABC. They didn't get it, and it was a real missed opportunity.

MEMORANDUM   ABC NEWS InterActive

David Bohrman
Executive Producer

To: Irwin Weiner
Date: February 26, 1990
Subject: The Future

The more conferences and meetings I've been taking part in lately concerning interactive technology, computers, video, etc, the more I am becoming convinced that we are on the eve of a major communications revolution. I'd like to briefly lay out what may be coming, and give some recommendations for things we at ABC can do to prepare. This is going to be substantial, and the profits associated with it could be very large.

The technologies of video, computers, television, cable and information retrieval are all converging. Within a few years, they will be so closely linked that they will, in fact, be all part of one beast. Take what cable and video rentals have done for the '80's, multiply it many times over, and you will get a sense of what I think will be commonplace by the end of the '90's: Everything will be on-line. Newsgathering may not change, but the way it gets distributed, and in fact, the way people watch television will.

As you know, whenever we speak and demonstrate what the InterActive unit is producing, we try to add that one day videodiscs will be obsolete and people will in the future connect directly 'to the basement of ABC News.' I am beginning to firmly believe that within just a few years this will actually begin to happen.

Imagine being at home, turning on your 'smart' TV, and selecting to watch last night's World News lead story, last month's Nightline, coverage of the Apollo 11 mission, environmental news since Earth Day, Martin Luther King's I have a Dream Speech, American Bandstand from 1964, an episode of the Avengers or Moonlighting, a stereo version of Star Wars, a Lincoln Center concert, the first Super Bowl, or the 1972 Olympics. I think that someday these and everything else that exists in film and video archives could actually be available, in real-time, to whomever wants to watch.... and for a fee.

The technologies that will make this possible are all very much under way. There are many small groups working on putting all of the pieces together already. The phone companies of the country desperately want to re-wire much or all of the US with fiber optic cable. Digital video storage schemes are evolving and are almost to the point of being usable right now. And WE (among others) have the content. And content will be the key to profits.

Last week in his keynote for a conference in California, John Sculley demonstrated an ABC News look at this future: ABC News InterActive On-Line. We produced a videodisc that simulated a glimpse of what you might be able to do with this technology. It was extremely successful, and provoked much thought and discussion.

This is going to happen. We have the opportunity to grab this concept, take charge of it, define it, make it happen, and make a great deal of money from it. But we must not let others do all these things first. There's plenty of room down this road for all who have content to be viewed, but there's no reason we shouldn't grab as much as possible.

I don't know anyone who's smart enough to really know how to deal with these possibilities. But I think there are a couple of early steps we can take to position ourselves for the time when we can really seize an initiative in this area.

1 Buy any film or video archive that becomes available.
   (or quietly seek out other archives that have material we want to own.)
   - These need not be just news related. As ABC/Capital Cities, we should expect to have entertainment, sports, music, and motion picture archives that can be put on-line with all the rest of what we have. People will not go to the corner video rental store in this brave new world.... They will choose what they want to see from a menu on the TV and expect to see it instantly.

2 Begin to forge alliances with others.
   - We need to work with companies who will make connecting to and receiving information from our storage centers easy (like phone companies), companies researching and building digital video storage systems (like phone companies, too), and television manufacturers (like Sony, which is getting involved in all of this via the HDTV route).

3 Think about InterActive (with reasonable R & D money and some goals) forming the nucleus for what could eventually become another publishing division of either ABC or Cap Cities. Eventually the division wants to draw from, but not be limited to news material.

4 Raise the awareness of the public about what we are currently doing. We are a wonderful alternative to Whittle's Channel One. We are the leaders in interactive videodiscs for education. We've already got five products on the market (both consumer and educational, in both the US and Japan.) We have a television network at our disposal. We should figure out a responsible, and effective way to use it.

We have already begun to be contacted by some of the groups working to make all of these things happen. I got a call just yesterday from a Senior Technologist at SouthWest Bell who wants to build a small fiber-optic demonstration of the new information-retrieval technologies.

Although this memo is just a general overview of what may lie ahead, I can provide you with specifics about who is doing what to bring all of this to reality.

I suppose that all of this sounds pretty ambitious, and some pretty far-fetched. But I have seen many preliminary parts of these developments. There are obstacles, and I suppose nothing is without risk. But I really think the only question is 'When?' not 'If?'

DB

You are obviously the embodiment of someone who believes in the cross-fertilization of different knowledge streams and the 'un-siloing' of education. You bring this cross-fertilization into the soil of what you are working on and, frankly, it makes a great mulch. It seems to me this is not just imperative in innovation, but is also imperative in the industry you're in.

Correct, yes. It's about diversity... the diversity of ideas and experiences.

How frustrated have you been during your career in trying to move forward with these innovative thoughts when, for instance, you were laughed off when you came forward with your 'future' document?

Well, you just sort of keep doing it, you know. ABC news could have owned much of new media had we done it, but they didn't go that way and the world evolved. I tried to bring some of those same ideas to NBC... a couple stuck but....

Unfortunately I had to produce every live minute of the O J Simpson trial at NBC.... I was planning the coverage and knew about QuickTime VR, which was just about to come out of Apple. I arranged to rent the crime scene for the Simpson case, hire a photographer and took, let's say, 15 or so nodes of pictures. So we had a couple of hundred photos that were in a bunch of 3D scenes, used by our legal correspondent Jack Ford. While we were on the air live, he was able to do what, basically, you'd call street view if you're on Google maps, for the crime scene in Simpson's house. We built that in 1995.

When I became Washington Bureau Chief at CNN, not only did I run the Washington bureau but I had oversight of all special events and all the news gathering and programmes in Washington. I had budgetary responsibility over a series of budgets and I knew that, if I stayed within budget, I could make spending decisions. This was how I was able to buy a Magic Wall and devote some resources to create the hologram. I was lucky not to have to ask permission for everything that I did.

> *Those responsible for innovation, for exploration, for R&D, for imagining possible futures, are like the testicles of a corporation: they fire out lots and lots of ideas, not all of which are going to grow to fruition, but to do that need to be close to, but not inside, the corporate body politic. In order to accept successful innovation from inside, innovation has to be believed in and given room and resources to grow and to fail.*
>
> *Innovation is inherently about transformation and experimentation. To unpick the assumptions requires space from the daily implementation of those assumptions, a willingness to listen to other people's ideas, to embrace the weird, to treat everyone as equals, and imagine your own obsolescence.*
>
> *Fear crushes innovation. Micro-managers, endless divisions and departments, competitive [rather than collaborative] reviews and rewards, internal politics, unclear roles, reporting and responsibilities, cronyism and a culture of fear – these make innovation impossible.*
>
> **Faris Yakob** (Award-winning strategist and creative director, writer and public speaker)

You could get away with asking for forgiveness rather than permission if it didn't work out.

Yes, sort of; and, there are some other realities. What I did worked out pretty well.

I have a patent. If you look at [it] – I'm not going to tell you I invented non-linear editing... but look at the patent... it's basically non-linear editing. We had the hypercard system, that grew into this interactive video unit using laser discs at ABC News... we came up with something I called the Documentary Maker where you could rearrange video segments and pick new 'ins' and 'outs' and the computer would automatically play them back in the order you decided, not the order they actually were on the disc... which is essentially non-linear editing.

We applied for a patent at ABC. We got it but, despite a lot of pushing by me that we should actually get out there and enforce and build it, it fell into neglect. It was basically abandoned – although I tried to resurrect it a couple of times – [but] it is cited in a lot of other patents from Abbott and Sony and other non-linear editors.

You mentioned the hologram and the Magic Wall, and you were the instigator of the YouTube debates. All three of them have shaped electioneering and the involvement of different demographics during election night and the election process.

They're all sort of linked and spread over years as [they] wove together and ended up being what they were.

Let's say I've got all this news-producing, new media stuff that happened in the very late 80s and early 90s. Then, hop over to NBC where a director and I began to learn a lot about virtual sets because it was all the rage, and it still is.

Virtual sets worked somewhat but weren't spectacular because they looked a little cheesy. In mid-95 we travelled around the world and learnt a lot about high-end rendering and virtual sets, thinking, on election night, we might want virtual capitol, virtual graphics or highly rendered things. I quickly realized that a virtual set is like a flight simulator: it draws, in real time, something as realistic as you can, depending on how fast the computer is. The first thing I did at NBC is make a virtual Bosnia, because Bosnia was in the news. We made our own fly-over capability that could happen live, in real time on TV.

Shortly after that, NBC announced it was going to create MSNBC, the cable channel. I did several things as part of the start-up, but the one that touches here is that I created a show called 'The Site' with Soledad O'Brien; we built the facility and had a virtual character using an Onyx and Leo Laporte – who's really well-known in the tech world – in a motion suit, off camera. The character, Dev Null, was the barista in the espresso bar on the set that we had. He would answer questions and be rendered in real time… it was like a cartoon character interacting with Soledad. It was at that point, in 1996, I knew that at some point I could replace the virtual character with a live video. It took me 15 years to do it, and it proved to be very complex, but it planted the seed for the hologram.

I was [also] the CEO of a company called Pseudo. In 2000 we did the first live streaming from a political convention, in Philadelphia. Pseudo went bankrupt when the internet went bust but [it] was very much user-generated, user-interactive streaming. I think if Pseudo had gotten in earlier, and had the economy been better, we would have ended up being YouTube. It was streaming, real-time, social media interaction – which was critical as things evolved.

So finally I'm back at CNN and I want to do mapping and real-time things and I went to a... basically a trade show for spies called Geoint. It's a non-classified trade show for the remote-sensing, satellite imagery community. I went looking for new display technologies and that's where I found the Magic Wall. We were just getting started on the Primary coverage, so we moved it to New York, I married John King to it and it evolved.

For the 2004 election I wanted to do an electronic version of the way it looked in the 50s and 60s and I had this idea of doing it at the NASDAQ. The head of the network thought it was crazy but he said, 'Go ahead and try.' And we ended up doing election night in 2004 from the floor of the NASDAQ with 72 screens. It was very complicated to traffic them and to put words and video in them, but it was a proof of concept that, I think, led to the TV show at CNN called 'The Situation Room', which led to all of CNN's coverage with the big walls and graphics. So much of television has now adopted these big walls of graphics in an election and for daily news coverage – on CNN and almost anywhere else.

As we were rehearsing for 06, Eric Schmidt from Google came by for a little tour. He was a big CNN fan, and said to me, 'Whatever Google can do for you, let me know.' Leap forward about a year, and I'm in the office of Jon Klein the then president of CNN. I had some interesting ideas about the structure and format for debates; and he said, 'I got to go for two minutes to talk to someone outside. When I come back let's talk about how we can get some user-generated ideas into the conversation.' So, in two minutes, I actually came up with the YouTube debates.

In that two-minute period, it hit me that we could have a debate where all of the questions would be asked by people, none of them reporters. When he came back from his two-minute meeting I threw out this idea. (Although it seems a no-brainer today, it was a 'brainer' at the time.) Jon loved it. I got back to Eric Schmidt, because they had bought YouTube, and connected with the YouTube people who were itching for something to do. We talked to the political parties.

The Democratic Party was really interested to do something with new media and ended up sanctioning our debate as the first official debate of the 2008 campaign; that became the Democratic YouTube debate. And the Republicans needed to do that as well.

That sort of changed debates. Who knows how it's going to evolve, but I think the people who are out there in the country will always have some role in getting questions to people who are running for president.

For the 2008 election, the graphics required to do real-time 3D were much better and cheaper. That's when I threw out the idea of trying to do the hologram idea. Editorially, it wasn't hugely significant, but I think it was a really interesting step in the evolution of television.

If you go way back to when I started at ABC, I was part of 'Nightline'. One of the things I did was live coverage, from Mount Everest, of a climb. Ted [Koppel] hated it at the time. When he retired from 'Nightline', Wolff [Blitzer] had Jeff Greenfield and me in the Situation Room to talk with Ted. I brought it up and he said, 'Well David, what I thought, when you said live coverage, is that there's nothing to see... maybe a cloud will float by. What you saw was that, if we could do live coverage from Mount Everest – the most remote place on the planet – there's nothing to stop us from going anywhere with live and immediate coverage of news.'

It's the same thought that I have on the hologram; it's a glimmer of what I know we're going to be able to do and it won't be anywhere near as complicated. It drew a great amount of attention; it was quite fun and sort of spectacular. It was important at that level, but not editorially important for the story.

CNN, in and of itself, was quite a game-changer. In particular, when you look at the effect it had on, for instance, terrestrial news programmes. Do you see Current TV having the same kind of impact?

I don't know. We're both proud of, and hurt by, the fact that we're a small, independent channel. It's hard to punch through when you're not part of a conglomeration of 50 other networks that can co-promote you.

I'm pretty sure there's a lot of that to come in TV. But I honestly cannot tell you, right now, how Current will punch through and make a mark or if it will end up in someone's DNA and get transferred on. [This interview was conducted on 14 December, approximately three weeks prior to Current TV being sold to Al Jazeera, the Qatar-based news broadcaster.]

You've had a bird's eye view of the evolution of television and new media. And I note that your father was renowned for his investigative reporting, a skill that seems to be currently less prevalent. What are your thoughts on how to re-engender an appetite for it?

I actually think that that is on the rebound. I think that it was a very fertile period in the sort of immediate post-Watergate era. The networks were not seen then as profit centres but instead as sort of civic responsibilities. CBS News had CBS Reports, NBC had their white papers and ABC did as well. It really hit a peak at Watergate and post-Watergate. And then, when the profit margin of news became critical, it began to disappear.

I think you're now seeing that it is so much easier and cheaper, and so many people can create and edit this stuff, I think there'll be a rebound on it. We're certainly wanting to invest more in it. I think that there's a decent future there for people who have ideas, see stories, and want to tell them. With the web and the technologies that are there today, it's much easier to punch through. Ideas can bubble up and there's a lot more chance for people who want to tell those stories or make those docs or do those investigations.

Are you working on a particular project right now?

We just sort of did version 1.0 and 1.5 of true user-generated television, with Current and the conventions and election night. The way I explained it to our web team was: other people have put Twitter on the screen, at the bottom. But I had a picture of a glass of champagne with all the bubbles in. I said, 'Imagine every single one of those bubbles is a conversation taking place in the world and, somehow, you know what those conversations are about and you can join in and jump from one to another and participate in them.' The explanation actually worked and that's what our online people created for Current.com during the election events....

We built a system and a structure where people on our website could, almost in a three-dimensional way, get a digital sense of the conversations going on in the world via Twitter – we've confined it to Twitter for now – and they could float around, look into those conversations, dive in and participate and interact with other people.

I think a cross-platform sharing of user interaction is a major cornerstone for Current; and we're beginning to think about where that goes. More of our programmes are in that kind of environment all the time. It will be a challenge for TV; there are a lot of technological challenges there but it's not necessarily the Twitter world that's going to decide how this evolves. It's going to be people and where they get the most interaction and satisfaction from using these tools.

" There are lots of definitions out there and some of them are very neat and tidy. I personally think trying to define something like innovation is a bit like trying to define creativity. If you put it into a box, or summarize it into a series of characteristics, it seems likely that you will end up missing it and creating limitations around something that inherently has to break boundaries and be indefinable.

I know we need to know more about innovation, so we can do it better and more often. But perhaps we should be focusing on the diversity of different conditions or circumstances this happens in rather than trying to define what innovation is. This way, it would seem, we can start to understand how to allow it or encourage it to happen rather than what is supposed to emerge, or what it looks like when it does.

James Gardiner (Globally-renowned thought leader in innovative construction techniques)

Keyword imagination exercise

Take a few minutes to close your eyes, relax and explore these keywords. You may want to make a note of any ideas that emerge that you want to explore later.

Alliance, Evolve, Information, Online, Public

Seth Godin

Seth has written 14 bestselling books that have been translated into more than 30 languages. Deemed 'America's greatest marketer', he is the writer of one of the most popular blogs on the net. His Kickstarter campaign for his latest book, *The Icarus Deception*, broke records for its size and the speed that it reached its goal. Seth has founded dozens of companies, most of which failed. However, Yoyodyne, his first internet company, which was acquired by Yahoo! in 1998, pioneered Permission (online) Marketing. His latest company, Squidoo.com, raises money for charity and pays royalties to its million-plus members.

Your latest book, *The Icarus Deception*, is a 'next-step' in the innovation of the publishing industry, and a great example of how to thrive in the connection economy. You've noted that the point of the project is, 'organizing the tribe and persuading the book publishing world to step up and do a serious job of retail work...' with attention and connection as joint goals. To what end?

To bring books that matter to people who want to read them. It makes no sense at all to let the jumble of the bookstore, or the long tail of the net, have wonderful books disappear.

In one of your blog posts, you note that Nicola Tesla was 'ridiculed, marginalized and ignored,' and there is no doubt that he was outshone by the marketing and business savvy of the likes of Thomas Edison. Do you think that 'Tesla-types' can have a different experience using tools such as the web, as they can reach the 'tribe' directly, rather than needing a corporate machine to do so?

There's no doubt that the lack of choke points and filters make it ever more likely that effective ideas surface. They don't always look like break-throughs, until they change everything.

If you look at most e-Cloud economic models, they seem to be largely based on an extension of interruption marketing and trawling data. What innovation do you think is necessary to provide the type of capability that you have proposed with permission marketing?

Well, Dropbox for example is 100 percent viral plus permission. No hard-sell, no spam. The net is about sharing, and the Cloud magnifies that.

Do you envisage a publishing industry that may lose its need for publishers?

Publishing and printing are very different things, of course. Publishing is about the taking of risks to bring new ideas to readers. Well, the net does a great job of turning all of those needs completely upside down. I don't think we lose intermediaries, but I'm very sure it's a different set of skills.

What skill-set is needed to retrain existing executives to move their minds and companies successfully into the digital economy?

The ones that haven't moved their minds already, on their own, are going to have to be scared straight, which is a shame, because that leads to a lot of pain and dislocation as industries disappear.

Is there a set of tools or a path that you would recommend readers embark upon to gain this insight?

For sure; the simplest, most obvious and most important thing to do is go. Start. Do it. Put yourself out there. On weekends or evenings, but go. If you don't do it, you can't understand it.

> *Core innovation is key – interestingly enough, being the innovator is really important – but sometimes being an innovator is not necessarily inventing, it is being able to actually innovate – to build... to execute.*
>
> **Linda Jenkinson** (Chairman and co-founder of LesConsierges Inc)

Keyword imagination exercise

Do, Permission, Share, Tribe, Viral

Gerd Leonhard

Gerd Leonhard is a renowned futurist and author, provocative keynote speaker, think-tank leader and adviser, and international thought leader in topics as varied as digital business models, social media, consumer trends, entrepreneurship, branding, copyright advertising and IP protection.

Photo credit: F Ammann

You are internationally renowned for the workshops you lead and the keynote speeches you present to a wide range of businesses at the Tier One level. That said, Tier One companies are not necessarily thought of as being innovative. Can you train the employees and management within these organizations to think more innovatively or is that trying to push too large a rock up too steep a hill?

I wonder about that. Milton Freeman talked about crisis being the cause of change. I think it's pain or love; this is a human factor. I don't think we change until we have the need to do something urgently; we don't have enough foresight to do what is [necessary] pre-emptively, in most cases.

Steve Jobs was obviously driven by something completely different than calculating return on investment or listening to focus groups.

One of the things keeping [certain] companies away from innovation is that they don't make any room for it; they expect people to act like machines, fulfil their roles and make money. The paradox is: the more obsessed you are with making money, the less you'll make, because it prevents you from realizing opportunities. One of the big issues with the stock market in general is that it drives us to a perception that everything is about the immediate bottom line.

This short-term thinking is one of the things I talk to my clients about. My clients are all really different. What I do for them is speak on these issues to their clients. They use me as a way of saying things that they would like to say, but can't.

Your new book, *From Ego to Eco* has quite a tag line: *Why business as usual is killing us, and what to do about it*. It certainly speaks to issues that most businesses are having to deal with – or certainly will have to face sooner rather than later. One of these issues, which I believe is having a massive impact, is enduser empowerment.

I think that a lot of companies are perceiving the empowerment of consumers as a pain in the butt. Because, for them, the idea of having a monopoly, or less transparency, is much better for businesses because you don't have to deal with the conversation. If you can sell your stuff by having a monologue, like phone companies or banks did, then it's much better. You get much less feedback [from] pesky users. But [consumer empowerment is] inevitable and happening everywhere.

I think another inevitability is the empowered consumer/enduser realizing that their attention is worth something. And, this attention economy will undoubtedly change the business paradigm. This is quite clearly the 'currency' that the user has and [is] using already. We're basically extorting value out of Facebook and Google in return for our attention and we will be very picky as to what they do.

For example, we get to use all the cool Google stuff for free; in return they're tracking us. Eventually, I think this will lead to 5 billion people making pretty heavy demands on some of these services and it may backfire in the sense that, in a few years, we will prefer to just pay. But, rather than pay with our attention, we'll pay money. I can imagine a Facebook version where I would pay to keep it clean, without all the ads. But this is, of course, the nature of capitalism. At some point in the future, for those companies, the money will become more important than the user.

> " *I think there is also a thing with innovation where we do understand enough about what it takes – time, freedom, imagination, money, perseverance, failure, etc but few people want to actually do what it takes, like staying healthy or becoming enlightened, so instead they keep looking for a short cut or an easier way.*
>
> **J D Lasica** (Founder of Socialmedia.biz and Socialbrite)

You are a futurist, a musician, a multi-linguist and an expert in many varied fields. How does this cross-fertilization of expertise empower you?

You know, it's fairly trivial to scoop up lots of data, read reports and be smart in that sense. It's like having a Wikipedia implant. But that's just data.

The human brain is very good at recognizing patterns and putting stuff together that's not logically connected. I try to combine what I get from my research and what I get from talking to my clients. I derive patterns from this. Some of these are turned into memes, which are universal guidelines like: 'data is the new oil' or 'paying with attention' – those stories that are true across all industries.

I use a lot of metaphors, for instance we're going from selling copies to selling access. This relates to the fact that we're not going to have physical money or credit cards, we're going to sell access to money on our mobile devices. Rather than carrying it, we'll have a way of delivering it electronically.

The good thing about being a futurist or somebody who looks at different domains is that, hopefully, you can recognize patterns across those domains and you can add value by being an outsider.

I note that you won the Quincy Jones award in 1985.

That's how I started. I've been playing music since I was 10 and had an interesting career in jazz and world music.

Could it be that simply gathering data is the equivalent of reading sheet music and the extrapolation of that data, and what you do with those extrapolations is the equivalent of playing jazz with the information?

Absolutely. It's a long-known fact that musicians have the ability to improvise and translate to other sectors. This analogy is actually quite good because a robot could play music... and some musicians that are classically-trained don't add variations. They have to play what's on the paper.

Business is, in a way, an art of some sort because if it was just about facts it would be easy. If we're talking about innovation, the innovation is not in learning lots of stuff then turning facts into money; it's creating something new out of the things that you've seen.

You are based in Europe, in a multicultural society on a multicultural continent; is that important when we talk about innovation?

Innovation is a virtual country with virtual citizens. It exists everywhere, but we have cultural issues. In Western countries, especially in Europe, we're rich and that success makes us lazy.

In countries [where] people are hungry, they don't care about conventions in the sense of who does what. Business traditions are much less ingrained and they have a reason to innovate, because they have to get out of the hole that many of them are still in. Be it because they're not making enough money or they're not changing their environment enough, they have reasons and, therefore, they have a culture of innovation.

Culture is really important to foster innovation... a culture of allowing people to make mistakes, to accept failure, which we don't do in Germany. In Germany failure means you're tarnished.

And yet, Germany has a successful economy.

That's true, the Germans are great at production. They invent better processes so they are very good at [making] things like cars, airplanes and trains, stuff that has to be produced well. But are they good at reinventing the way the world works? No – that's Silicon Valley and China.

In America, everybody wants to change the world and say: 'I have invented the nuclear power plant that fits in a baseball.' They are going to invent stuff that changes the world. How far you dare to go and how much you risk has to do with how much you have to lose or to gain.

Perhaps one of your roles is to embolden your clients and stop them from being frightened to take risks.

There's a certain chemistry that is required for innovation. I try to create opportunities for some sort of osmosis of ideas. The issue with academic innovation is that it's based on facts, factoids, research and numbers; it's not being creative, it's just creating a plan. And in this world – because this is the age of creative destruction – it's not about making plans. It's about sticking your finger into the flow and coming up with something that is a fit for that situation, at that time.

> *Innovation is the daily practice of fusing creativity with problem solving. It is the way we grow as human beings, find solutions to large-scale problems and ultimately build a better world.*
>
> **Claire Diaz-Ortiz** (Author and speaker, leading social innovation at Twitter, Inc)

So it's not just jazz; it's improvisational jazz.

Of course improvising is at the core of all these things. Everybody knows: if you're in business it's never going to be what you thought it would be. We're living in an age of permanent beta, so whatever your business model is, you can bet somebody is going to take a shot at it next week.

Apple is now one of the most valuable companies in [history]. They didn't have a carefully researched battle plan, like Microsoft did; Steve Jobs just followed his own obsession. That's a tall order. We have to realize that people like this are not there because they have a careful plan or they're super smart. They just have this really original mix of tenacity and an egocentric world view that leads them to take over.

So do you think those uber-innovators are born rather than made?

Well, they're made in the sense of their socialization. Clearly, that was the case for Steve Jobs. But the ability to innovate can be trained in the sense that the blocks can be removed.

The brain is a plastic organism; it changes. When you're constantly doing a certain task, the brain just finds that to be normal. When you change that task, the brain can find another way of doing things to be normal. But you have to make that change in the way that you think.

Also, creating the need for innovation is crucial... by creating a pressure point or a 'love point', so to speak, you fall in love with an idea. Jeff Bezos fell in love with his idea of the Kindle and he staked the entire company on it. And there was no proof whatsoever that anybody wanted it. Innovation cannot be derived from some rational mix of data where you say: all data points here, so let's do it. That's not the way it works.

" I define innovation as 'something different that has impact'. The two key words are 'something' and 'impact'. 'Impact' reminds us that innovation is distinctly different from its precursors – creativity and invention. Those things are important, no doubt, but until you translate a creative spark into an idea that generates profits, improves a process, or addresses some other problem, you have not innovated. 'Something' reminds us that innovation is not consigned to white-labcoat-wearing scientists toiling away in laboratories. Innovation isn't the job of a few people in the organization. Everyone should be thinking about new ways to solve old problems. Innovation goes well beyond new products and services to include new marketing approaches, new processes, new organizational structures, even new leadership behaviours.

One example I highlight in The Little Black Book of Innovation *is how a librarian at CNN named Lizzie Jury assembled pre-verified facts on important topics in the news into 'Fast Facts' on the company intranet, making them instantly accessible to journalists. This had real impact – allowing journalists to get the information they needed faster, smoothing the library's utilization, and allowing the team to go even deeper when needed. It is a great example of an 'everyday innovation' launched not by Mark Zuckerberg or Richard Branson, but a humble middle manager inside a large organization.*

Scott Anthony (Managing Partner at Innosight, Chairman of the IDEAS Ventures Investment Committee)

Keyword imagination exercise

Consumer, Deliver, Demand, Enduser, Feedback

Final thoughts

The immediacy and incessant reach of media is now so refined and defined in its ability to be individually tailored it can truly be described as me-dia – with a distinct disposition that is almost wholly dependent upon who is viewing it. Industries such as publishing that were until recently seen as, if not sacrosanct then certainly inviolable, are in a fight for their lives. If they endure they will certainly bare scars from a hard-fought battle for survival.

Another battle continuing to rage is for the heart of an independent me-dia; one that is not hamstrung by censorship, partisanship and propaganda. Just as empowered endusers have the ability and wherewithal to create their own sources of news via online blogs, news feeds, etc, they also have the capacity to demand a me-dia that provides them with reporting that is thorough, deepened by contextual understanding and seasoned with experience and empathy. It remains to be seen whether they will do so.

Being grounded when the sky's the limit

07

Benefit, Child,
Cooperate, Courage,
Danger, Dream, Engage,
Explore, Facilitate, Fool, Freedom,
Future, Games, Guide, Imagine, Journey,
Mentor, Mistake, Motivate, Need, Perspective, Play,
Question, Scar, Strategy, Tenacity, Use, Variation, Wisdom

If William Pitt the Elder, British Prime Minister from 1766 to 1778, was correct in his statement, 'Unlimited power is apt to corrupt the mind of those who possess it', it may do us good to think what effect unlimited access to innovative tools and technologies will have on us as individuals and as a society. Will the potential to be online and constantly connected – perhaps by wearing 'Google goggles' in your every waking moment – enhance our lives or decimate our ability to have meaningful, person-to-person, encounters? Should we aim to learn how to play well and wisely, not just with each other but with technology and innovation? Will we become more connected to these things in a spiritual sense, as our physical, emotional and economic connection with them evolves? These are not 'black and white' easily answered questions but they are, perhaps, ones that should give us pause as we hurl ourselves headlong towards our great, innovative future together.

What is without question is that innovations should empower not enslave. As such, it is up to empowered endusers to decide for themselves how 'on' they want to be and to have the strength and wherewithal to turn off when they choose to – or need to.

> I take off on the weekends. I completely unplug from technology and it has changed my life. It's been three years and it allows me to do all that I do during the weekends. I'm a very present mother and present with myself and my husband. It really is an amazing experience to do it every week.
>
> **Tiffany Shlain**, multi-award-winning filmmaker,
> founder of The Webby Awards, and co-founder
> of the International Academy of Digital Arts and Sciences.

It is also incumbent upon them to make their voices heard with regards to what tools they want and need – both personally and professionally. Just as empowered citizens vote politically, empowered endusers can vote with their wallet – the best way to punish those companies that aren't innovating with you in mind is to avoid purchasing their products, technologies and tools.

Ease of use is a must in the new GDE. If a new tool or innovative technology is to have any chance of becoming internationally ubiquitous it must be simple to use. Assuming that users are interested in programming, reading instruction manuals and understanding the 'tech behind the tool' is a death knell for a technology – at least one that hopes to be used by millions of users, be they consumers or employees.

The innovation that may have the greatest effect on us as individuals, communities, countries and continents may be 3D printing – or 'additive manufacturing' to use its correct name – which 'builds' things by printing off minute layer after minute layer of material. It is possible that, whether you know it or not, you already own something that has been created by this technology. It is not all-pervasive yet... but it is well on its way.

It is said that if you can draw your idea, you can 3D print it. Simple blueprints can be developed with easily accessible software, which can be tweaked with the click of a mouse to create a design specific to individual wants and needs – no matter how banal or bizarre. You can print a replica foetus or Formula 1 car and, potentially, for the hungry carnivore, meat products. Yes, meat – to eat. Currently focused on leather products, a company in Missouri is exploring bio-printing with a view to moving into printing edible meat products. The question: 'How do you want your steak?' may have an entirely new connotation soon.

In Chapter 4 we explored some of the ways that 3D printing can be used to save lives. The fact that it can be used to print guns is proof, if it were needed, that the technology can also be used to create tools that can take lives. As the technology advances and the requisite components become smaller and more affordable – not unlike the evolution of mobile phone technology – it doesn't take a great leap of imagination to see this innovation as part of every wired household. The ramifications for this are many. For instance, if it is possible for anyone to print a gun, what will that mean to gun control laws? How will it affect the retail industry if ever-demanding customers can order exactly what they want directly from an industry-sized 3D printer or make it themselves from the printer they keep at home?

Personal 3D printers are now small enough to fit into a suitcase. Already they're priced so you can purchase a basic 3D model for approximately US$350 – and like the early mobile phones, prices will continue to fall far and fast. Along with easing prices, the printers will surely become simpler to set up and will soon be servicing communities and individuals all around the world.

These changes will obviously impact economies at local, national and supranational levels and they will do so in a multitude of ways. Just as the Spinning Jenny altered the textile industry – and was a central component of the Industrial Revolution – and desktop publishing altered the printing industry, 3D printing will forever change the manufacturing industry. It will lower the cost of living as the price of certain items falls dramatically; but just as surely it will put swathes of skilled and semi-skilled workers out of work.

The unskilled labouring jobs, which have been sent offshore, will have less relevance in 3D-adjusted economies. The economy surrounding 3D printing is likely to be more skilled rather than less – which leads to a need for more education, more apprenticeships, more training, all of which flow into and through the knowledge based GDE. The potential is there to shift the trade balance between East and West, but also between the Majority World and the rest of the world as 3D printing enables and empowers local control and diversity.

There is likely to be no industry or individual unaffected in some way by what could become an unprecedented period of upheaval. We noted in Chapter 4 that it is already possible to print limbs for people of any age, but it is a particularly economical practice for children who are in need of replacement limbs: children grow quickly and, as with their shoes, they will outgrow their limbs sooner rather than later. With a few tweaks to a software-created blueprint, a new limb – and new shoes for that matter – can be printed at a fraction of the current costs.

Housing crisis; what housing crisis? It's not just furniture and fixings that can be produced: innovators such as Enrico Dini are working on printing entire buildings. This is an innovation that won't just alter home and business, it will also affect our environment. The components are certainly recyclable, thus less pollution and fewer landfills. It could also affect air pollution levels as items that currently have to be shipped halfway around the world can be 3D printed locally – quickly, easily and economically. Though we are unlikely to be able to print our way out of climate change, printing is being used to create sustainable reefs by using 3D models, already sunk off the coast of Bahrain and soon, hopefully, being used to engender growth on the Great Barrier Reef.

Undoubtedly 3D printing will bring to mind, for science fiction fans at least, 'Star Trek' replicators. One can only wonder how the technology can be used by those looking to explore and, some might say, exploit space. Closer to home, perhaps we'll be able to exploit this innovation and, rather than rely on current service providers, we'll be able to 3D print a small satellite and play with bandwidth that is ours alone.

D-Shape printing, in its endless variations, will give mankind a new method to shape the world over the coming centuries by mimicking nature.

Enrico Dini, international thought leader
in developing D-Shape, 3D printing building technology

INTERVIEWS

William (Bill) Storage

An aerospace engineer by training, William (Bill) Storage is a thought leader and innovator in software architecture, systems engineering and design strategy. He is a sought after and successful CTO, entrepreneur, speaker, teacher, historian and cave explorer. As well as being an avid photographer, he is a major innovator in photographic lighting and equipment, which is brought to the fore in his work in archaeological sites and the world's deepest caves. He is a Visiting Scholar at the Center for Science, Technology, Medicine and Society at the University of California, Berkeley.

It could be said that you are an 'innovator's innovator', Bill, in that you have an extremely broad and wide set of experiences and expertise which you bring to your initiatives. How important has innovation been to you?

I was schooled as an engineer, a discipline that is fundamentally concerned with product and process innovation, so it's been rather central for me, and will continue to be so.

Almost all businesses identify innovation as a priority, but despite the attention given to the topic, I think we're still struggling to understand and manage it. I feel like the information age – communications speed and information volume – has profoundly changed competition in ways that we haven't fully understood. I suppose every era is just like its predecessor in the sense that it perceives itself to be completely unlike its predecessors. That said, I think there's ample evidence that a novel product with high demand, patented or not, gets you a much shorter time to milk the cow than it used to.

Businesses – and hopefully our education system – are going to need to face the need for innovation (whether we continue with that term or not) much more directly and centrally, not as an add-on, strategy du jour, or department down the hall.

How do you define innovation?

Well, that term is a bit overloaded these days. I think traditionally innovation meant the creation of better or more effective products, services, processes and ideas. While that's something bigger than just normal product refinement, I think it pertained more to improvement of an item in a category rather than invention of a new category. More recently, the term seems to indicate new categories and radical breakthroughs and inventions. It's probably not very productive to get too hung up on differentiating innovation and invention.

Also, many people, perhaps following Clayton Christensen, have come to equate innovation with market disruption, where the radical change results in a product being suddenly available to a new segment because some innovator broke a price or user-skill barrier. Then suddenly, you're meeting previously unmet customer needs, generating a flurry of consumption and press, which hopefully stimulates more innovation. That's a perfectly good definition too.

> An innovation is anything new that radically changes the competitive landscape. An innovation may take the form of an idea, method, product, service, or process. True innovations are 'step changes' – they change your perception and expectation forever. For example, once you touch an Apple iPhone, you can no longer return to an older model of mobile phone interaction. Even if the product doesn't survive, the knowledge of what has been done differently lives on. Also, innovation is both a process and outcome. In my work I focus on the process in order to improve innovation outcomes, addressing repeatability, organizational awareness and team formation.
>
> **Tamara Carleton** (Founder and CEO of Innovation Leadership Board LLC)

I suppose neither of those definitions really captures the essence of the iPhone, which I would consider a great example of successful innovation, despite really being 'merely' a collection of optimizations of prior art. So maybe we should expand the definitions to include things that improve quality of life very broadly or address some compelling need that we didn't previously know we had – things that just have a gigantic 'wow' factor.

There's also room for seeing innovation as a new way of thinking about something. That doesn't get too much press, but I think it's a fascinating subject that interacts with the other definitions, particularly in the sense that there are sometimes rather unseen innovations behind the big visible ones. Some innovations are innovations by virtue of spurring a stream of secondary ones.

This cascade can occur across product spaces and even across disciplines. We can look at Galileo, Kepler, Copernicus and Einstein as innovators. None were plodding, analytical types. All went far out on a limb, in defiance of conventional wisdom, often with wonderful fusions of empiricism and wild creativity.

In 1962, Thomas Kuhn, a historian of science at UC Berkeley, proposed a radically innovative way to look at scientific revolutions caused by these innovators. Kuhn's term for this model is ubiquitous: 'paradigm shift'. Kuhn was innovating about innovation, and his influence was global and enduring. He remains the most cited scientific author in history. But it doesn't stop there. Kuhn's innovative view of innovation was adopted – often horribly misapplied, from his perspective – by all sorts of other disciplines, including a variety of business management philosophies and product and business innovation methodologies. 'Design thinking' is one of them. It has been a boon to innovative firms, Apple most famously.

Finally, we have to include innovations in government, ethics and art. They occasionally do come along. Mankind went a long time without democracy, women's rights or vanishing point perspective. Then some geniuses came along and broke with tradition – in a very rational yet revolutionary way that only seemed self-evident after the fact. They fractured the existing model and shifted the paradigm. They innovated.

Ultimately, the imperative for innovation is to improve people's lives, against the natural human instinct to resist change.

Mark Sanders (Engineer, designer, inventor and Managing Director of MAS Design Products Ltd)

Do you think that innovation, as a term, is being overused or oversold?

We have a problem in industry where we use these terms as if they are brands. But unlike brands, nobody is in control of them, so their meaning tends to drift and drift, usually not in a good way.

There's certainly nothing wrong with a variety of different people using the same term with different meanings as long as they recognize they're doing so. Innovation certainly suffers from meaning different things to different people, in the same conversation, who don't realize that they have different understandings of the term's meaning.

There is certainly an industry around selling the 'elixir' of innovation. And all of its derivatives and related flavours. 'Design thinking' and 'systems thinking' are two terms that go back several decades. Now both have been redefined to the point of meaninglessness, converted into strategic initiatives and sold as two-day seminars on how to rescue your company from whatever peril it faces. We have a problem there with credibility of terms; maybe it's ok if the term drifts away, so long as the concept remains.

Do you have a term that you prefer?

I don't. I just think that if you reduce the discussion about innovation, innovation management and fostering innovation to groups of terms, you're already in trouble.

It may also be that we, as human beings, can be lazy. So if someone comes to us with a group of boxes that need only to be ticked – and then we can call our company 'innovative'... well, that can be hard to resist.

It is hard for people to resist that. Traditionally, that problem you just described has been something that has plagued large businesses much more than small businesses. In big firms, you get what is called in the trenches: executive ass covering... Executives, unwilling to be accountable for decisions or strategic directions, call on a host of consultancies – basically to distribute the blame for a bad decision if the decision turns out to be bad. It's going to be a hard problem to get rid of as newer firms emerge as big companies.

Google and Facebook weren't on the map 10 years ago but Exxon and IBM were. Everybody expects that kind of behaviour in Exxon and IBM but all of these young employees who joined Google didn't expect that [ass covering] to happen. Now, I have no particular insider information into Google or Facebook and I don't mean to be picking on them. I'm just pointing out that, historically, this is a problem that plagues large organizations and I don't see any reason to exempt the new economy players from that.

> For years I felt intimidated working at NASA with 'rocket scientists'. I contributed quite a bit, but finally realized I [could] contribute to NASA's vision even more if I concentrated on my unique strengths. It is extremely important that we recognize the value in our varied perspectives and talents, our own potential, and the potential in each other. We all have the power to do great things.
>
> **Karen Freidt** (Lead for the Navigation Center for Creativity, Collaboration and Innovation at the NASA Langley Research Center)

Earlier you noted the big differences between large companies and small start-ups. That said, I would posit that multidisciplinary thinking is important in each of those types of organizations.

Probably so. I think that a small company doesn't have the luxury of excessive specialization or they don't even have the ability to do it. If you only have 10 employees, they are necessarily wearing multiple hats. Of course, it doesn't mean that they wear them well or that they come to the table with any preparation or background for the role that they've been thrust into.

I think we can do better in that area. We can call upon academia to ready us for these types of situations and larger businesses can do a better job of recognizing that these people have to function together. You see the word 'holism' kicked around a lot and that term might be a little bit too new age-y to gain a lot of credibility or have a lot of credibility in the right circles. But that may point us in the direction that we need to go. It doesn't need to be a 'touchy-feely' sort of thing. It could be a very concrete form of training and structure in businesses so that interdisciplinary teams can be functional.

Is it fair to say that the pursuit of the outcome using any and all available tools and knowledge is the hallmark of a great innovator rather than just using a particular academic or technical skill?

I certainly think so. If you look at the history of people who we consider great innovators a very large number of them are multidisciplinary in nature. The level of specialization we have now is a fairly recent phenomenon. If you look at really famous, creative, innovative people – Michelangelo for example – guys like him were trained or educated, perhaps self-educated but educated, in a wide variety of fields. They used that education, in combination with some form of slightly reckless determination, to get somewhere.

Some of the literature on innovation attempts to capture that but perhaps not in a way that really gives the young aspiring innovator much guidance. We can say, 'break rules and take risks' but that's rather meaningless if it's not your money that you're risking. And I don't think that characterizes the innovative and entrepreneurial spirit that the great innovators have very well. Certainly they were risk-takers but there's much more to it than that; it was a very rational and informed risk-taking in those cases.

Is it a genie that you can bottle? Is it something that can be taught or is it something that is innate?

Absolutely it can be taught. And if it can't be, we're in trouble, because we've got more and more demand for that finite number, if it is a finite number, of these creative yet rational geniuses. There is a need to develop these kinds of people, and a PowerPoint presentation, a seminar or an external corporate strategic initiative is not going to fit that bill.

> *More often than not, an innovative and disruptive idea, thought, product or practice tends to gain less recognition and support from outside at its first phase of development or improvement. This is the most critical stage when it comes to identifying 'something', which we believe cannot be missed as a 'seedling of innovation' that may grow for social change and impact, once provided appropriate 'nutrients in the right soil.'*
>
> **Hirofumi Yokoi** (Co-founder and President of the Akira Foundation)

Keyword imagination exercise

Take a few minutes to close your eyes, relax and explore these keywords. You may want to make a note of any ideas that emerge that you want to explore later.

Need, Perspective, Strategy, Teach, Wisdom

Zern Liew

Zern Liew juggles a lively combination of design, analysis and people skills to unravel complexity, enable light bulb moments, find ways through chaos, and turn ideas into truly useful (and beautiful) things. He has worked internationally on diverse projects across business processes, software applications and communications.

That you combine expertise in psychology and design must give you a broad perspective when it comes to understanding your clients and their needs. With that in mind, and noting your obvious use of multiple disciplines within your work, how powerful do you think multidisciplinary thinking can be for innovation?

Very, because the more perspectives and aspects you come into contact with, the more informed the possibilities. There's the game a lot of innovators play of drawing parallels: if you were a fish, what type of fish would you be? That sort of thing. If your business were a fast food chain rather than a medical clinic, what would you do? The wider your perspective across different industries, the more options will come up. It's like collecting weird facts… and it's helped me, personally, in getting forward.

So playing games enables innovation.

Absolutely. It's the idea of creative play… the constant shifting, back and forth, between the suspension of judgement and facing the cold hard facts before you. So why can't you, as a pharmaceutical company, behave as if you were selling McDonald's? If the group is able to play with that, it opens up possibilities.

That said, I'd imagine it's not uncommon for people to, in essence, glom together with others that they feel comfortable with – people who think like them and behave like them. Engineers may most enjoy working with engineers, and lawyers, perhaps, lean towards sticking with other legal minds.

You've hit it on the nail; this is one of the challenges in my work. People naturally coalesce into their own cliques and groups: these people think like me so therefore it will be easier to get up to speed with them. I feel more comfortable with them, they know what I'm talking about, so why would I want to talk with outsiders?

How is education, as it stands, preparing people for the 'great games' of the future?

Education, as I see it, is doing a great job of preparing people to work in the post-industrialized world of the last century. We're trained, as a society, to box people quickly into very clear-cut professions: you will be an accountant; you will be an engineer. But, will it prepare us for the future? I don't think so. And that's really, really frightening if you think about it too much.

You've written in the past about creative problem solving being an act of rebellion, which is a very evocative statement. I'd think that, in a hierarchical organization, there would be a level of fear around the word 'rebellion'. With that in mind, do you think there's something to be afraid of when looking at innovation from a management perspective?

Yes, because a lot of the words that are associated with innovation – and I don't mean innovation in that hollow marketing sense – are words like 'chaos', 'change', 'destroy', 'reinvent'. Those are all scary words because management is focused on reducing errors, reducing variation so they can keep making money.

If you moved that focus to building a balanced group that were empowered to bring innovative ideas forward, are there particular skill-sets that you'd want to ensure were covered off within that group?

I'd make sure that there were people representing each stakeholder group included. There would be a technical expert, a marketing person, a leader, a worker and maybe even a user of the product; all the different voices must have an opportunity to be expressed and heard. You also need a good facilitator, preferably someone from outside the group, to guide and challenge the thinking, to defuse any conflict, and maintain focus.

You can't be truly innovative unless you have a psychologically safe space; you need to respect people, listen to them and make sure they feel involved. You can't be truly innovative if you spend too much time being fearful or defending your territory.

For the last two years, I've been headed both formally and informally towards what Dan Pink described several years ago, as a 'freelance nation' style of working organization. Big companies are dead or dying, because infinite and predictable growth for big companies has always been difficult and is getting more difficult with the uncertainty in the world. So the future belongs to adaptable teams and, for me, those teams are loosely affiliated networks of professionals I've had the pleasure of knowing, primarily finding each other through LinkedIn, Twitter, etc, or those I know from having personally worked with them, or their colleagues, at one point or another.

So my innovative project, for all work I'm doing for the foreseeable future, is about assembling flexible teams that can do great work for clients that need the smartest people we can bring from around the world, and in whatever industry or domain experience is needed, to their problem. We don't necessarily need to formally be 100 percent full-time employees of the same firm – but when we're working together as 'corporate privateers', as my network partner Richard Platt calls this approach, we're 100 percent focused on bringing our expertise into sharp focus for our clients, and not just 'building a bench' or building a 'big company' for the sake of growth by itself.

Dan Keldsen (President of InformationArchitected.com
and co-founder of Level 50 Software)

> ### Keyword imagination exercise
>
> **Facilitate, Games, Guide, Reinvent, Variation**

Bill O'Connor

Bill O'Connor is the founder of the Innovation Genome Project, an initiative at Autodesk that is researching the top 1,000 innovations in world history with a view to extrapolating patterns and insights that can be applied today. He works in Autodesk's Corporate Strategy team and is the primary speechwriter for the company's CEO and CTO.

A recurring theme in these interviews is the necessity for courage – not fearlessness, which is thoughtless and uninformed – but courage in the face of knowing the great dangers and risks ahead, and going forward in spite of them.

True innovators, the ones who have gotten things done, will always have tell-tale scars and war stories. I don't like the army of consultants who talk about innovation as if they are experts at it. They can be very smooth, but often it seems like they haven't ever really pushed anything through against brutal opposition.

When I see someone without very apparent scars talking about 'innovation', I get a little suspicious. They may have read a lot about innovation, but they probably haven't been down in the trenches doing it.

I think you're right to be a little suspicious of salesmen talking about innovation, rather than innovators themselves.

You could argue that these innovation salesmen are like old-fashioned country preachers: their rap certainly has many of the aspects of a religious sermon and, also as with a religion, they don't have to prove anything either! Think about it: you can do an entire engagement with a Fortune 100 company, be paid millions of dollars as a consultant and still there might be nothing new or valuable that comes of it. You might be a member of the Army of IBNU: Interesting But Not Useful.

And speaking of interesting and useful, tell me about the Genome Project.

Autodesk's customers are designers, architects, engineers and digital artists in Hollywood's film and games industry. They have to be innovative, for real; they can't leave it as a theory because it's what they're paid for. That's why we think so much about innovation at Autodesk.

My idea was to study history's greatest 1,000 innovations, to find the patterns and the best practices that would really help people be actually innovative. So we're looking at everything from 'fire to Facebook'.

Every innovation goes through five phases: it's impossible; it's impractical, it's nearly possible; it's expected; and then it becomes required. It's like the Rosetta Stone for what things pass through.

We've had innovation for 2.6 million years; you could argue that the stone axe in Africa was the first innovation – I like to say it was invented by a woman, just to tweak the dudes in the audience. You know, some cave-woman said, 'Screw ripping this thing apart with my bare hands: I'll shape this rock so it's sharp and more useful to me!' This was the first innovation on earth...

My idea was to study those 1,000 innovations – get the patterns and the best practices and, from that, a genome. At this point we've looked at 200 innovations. What we found from our research is that – even if you don't know anything about 'innovation' – if you put a project or a challenge in the middle of a piece of paper or a whiteboard, and I ask you seven questions about it, you *will get* some really innovative ideas. These questions are the true DNA of innovation throughout history. We've codified the Seven Essential Innovation questions (using '**ILUMIAM**' as the mnemonic device), and people are using them to really great effect. They are:

I = What could you **Imagine** that would create a great experience for someone? Human flight is a great example of this, because it wasn't rational to expect we could do it, but we just *wanted* to do it.

L = What can we **Look** at in a different way? Jobs looked at a lot of things differently (technology, design, business, people, life), and because of this we've got iPhones, iPads, iTunes, etc.

U = What can we **Use** for the first time or in a different way? Steam-powered engines are a good example of this powerful innovation question.

M = **Move** is re-contextualizing in time or space. For instance, open innovation takes the innovation from only inside a company or organization, or even just one person's 'head', and moves it to both inside *and* outside those locations.

I = What can we **Interconnect**, or connect, that we're not connecting now? The printing press is a great example of this, because it's an innovation combining the wine press and the stamp punch. Edison also did this when he connected the light bulb to the electrical grid.

A = What can we **Alter** or change? This is a lot about the 'design' aspect of innovation. To use another Apple example, Steve Jobs altered the performance and design of what a smart phone (which already existed) was.

M = What can we **Make** or create that is completely new? The United States is a great example of something completely new, because it was the first country built on a set of principles rather than by tribal or purely historical forces.

Here's how I use the Seven Essential Innovation questions for consulting. I ask people: 'What's the biggest challenge/problem/opportunity in your company?' Then I put that in the centre of the whiteboard, ask these seven questions about it, and try to get three really great ideas per question. I usually end up with at least 21 ideas and, so far, 100 percent of the time people have been satisfied with both the quality and quantity of the ideas that have come up. And my response to that is that I'm not really surprised, because these are the same questions that innovators have been using successfully for millions of years.

> *There are two key shifts that are imperative for innovation to have the best chance of success within an organization: 1) a culture shift where innovation and innovator behaviour is inherent in the way business gets done; and 2) leveraging the world's resources external to the organization for new ideas, shared resources and risk, and knowledge becomes common practice.*

The greatest barriers to success come from resistance within the organization to do things differently such as connect externally to problem solve and generate new ideas. People by nature resist change and have been classically trained to problem solve internally within an R&D structure. Secondly, large organizations structurally can stifle innovation and people's thinking or ability to innovate. That's why we developed an open innovation 'catalyst team' to help our organization make these cultural and organizational changes.

Emily Riley (Connected Innovation
Catalyst for General Mills Worldwide Innovation Network)

Keyword imagination exercise

Courage, Danger, Required, Scars, Use

David Pensak

Dr David Pensak is a world-renowned innovator and entrepreneur. His career includes 30 years at Dupont, from which he retired in 2004 as their chief computer scientist. He was the inventor of the world's first business firewall, the Raptor System, which was bought by AXENT Technologies (now Symantec). David's innovative entrepreneurship and leadership continues with the Pensak Innovation Institute, his authorship of *Innovation for Underdogs*, and his work for the Centre for Interdisciplinary Innovation.

He is currently on the faculty of the George Washington University School of Law, the University of Delaware Business School and is Professor of Anaesthesiology at Drexel University College of Medicine.

In your book, *Innovation for Underdogs*, from which you are generously donating all proceeds to the Ronald McDonald House, you write about your first meeting with [Nobel Prize winner] Professor E J Corey at Harvard. It's a great story where you, as an undergraduate, don't wait to be invited to join his research group. Instead you explained to him that you were quite prepared and ready to join his group. With that in mind, how important do you think audacity is to an innovator?

It's vitally important. Unless you have real confidence in yourself you will be afraid of failure.

The best way I can illustrate that is with the concept of speed dating. I run sessions for speed innovation. I get a bunch of people together and each has one minute to talk to each of the other people in the group. At the end of the micro-interactions they have to decide who they want to partner with and write a plan. I've found that the more time they have to think about things, the more conservative and reticent they are in taking a risk. If you're audacious, you're much more likely to be innovative.

How debilitating is fear to the innovation process?

Some people find the innovation process terrifying, especially in corporate America where, these days, the reward for being innovative is you either lose your job or your carpool loses theirs.

All of us are genetically pre-wired for innovation; it's just about who has had the right teachers, or mentors, or the right internal courage to give himself permission.

How important has innovation been to your career?

It has been absolutely vital, as my career has been entirely directed towards creating, for my colleagues and my students, a world which goes well beyond thinking 'outside the box'. I reject that there could be, or should be, a box at all.

Innovation comes from needs, dissatisfactions, and curiosities. As the world becomes more homogeneous we will come to recognize requirements and opportunities all around the world. As an example, I have developed a way for the country of Jordan to generate geothermal power without water, because they are situated astride the Great African Rift, giving an extraordinary geothermal gradient. Professor Tony Flynn at ANU came up with a great way to purify water starting from cow manure, coffee grounds and clay. I have been extending his approach to larger scale systems, which could be useful in disadvantaged areas where there is no surplus power for purification systems.

Noting your work all over the world, with organizations such as the Innovative Economy Center, do you think that innovation has a nation?

Absolutely. If I had to pick the most innovative country in the world right now, it would be one of the poorest countries in South Eastern Africa. The social structure has men going off and doing whatever they feel like while the women have to find ways to feed their families on 30 cents a day. They are amazingly clever and resourceful because they have to be to feed their families. There's no network that they can lean upon, no infrastructure.

I've done some work, which is not yet published, where I look at religion as a correlation to innovation. What I've found is: if you believe in reincarnation you tend to be much more timid, for fear that if whoever does the ultimate judging doesn't like what you've done, you come back as a snail, or something like that. You think: I've always got a couple more lifetimes, so I'll do it then. Whereas in cultures where they don't believe in reincarnation, it's: what do I have to lose?

You've also put forward the opinion that innovation can be resented. Why do you think that's the case?

There's a bunch of reasons, but the biggest one is money. Often times the innovator winds up making a bunch of money and the people who surround him say, 'I could've done that;' or 'Why did he make so much money out of the deal?'

When I [invented] the firewall, I had an interesting challenge when it came to disposing of the stock after the IPO. I could've stayed in Delaware – and paid taxes on it, as if it was ordinary income – or move 10 miles away, to Pennsylvania, where it's taxed at just 2 percent. I moved to Pennsylvania and wound up getting a 12,000 square foot, 150-year-old house on 30 acres. The guy who was VP of my division at Dupont was infuriated by how much I made out of the deal, because he had to drive past my house every day on the way to work. After about six months, he said 'I really hate you' and I said, 'I didn't do anything.' 'Yeah,' he said, 'you were successful when I wasn't.'

The same might be said about your opportunity, as a child, to meet and 'play' with Albert Einstein. You didn't 'do anything' to get that opportunity, as he was a 'neighbour' and colleague of your father's, along with a number of other scientists at RCA. And yet, you certainly must have benefited from his – and their – proximity in some way.

Most of what I'm going to tell you is what I have gleaned from my parents, because I was only seven when he [Einstein] died. Apparently one day I was sitting in the sand box making a sand castle with him when it started to rain. I didn't want to go in as I was having too much fun, and yet my beloved sandcastle started to 'melt'. I said, 'Excuse me Doctor, why is this happening?' Rather than tell me what the answer was, he asked me a bunch of questions to help me figure out what was really going on. Like: what is sand made of? Why does sand stick together? Is there glue? Is it magnetism? By asking me questions that were specifically focused on what would most interest me as a child, I learnt how to analyse my world rather than being forced to analyse the world of adults before I was ready to appreciate the subtleties and implications of that.

Then there was Professor Seymour Bogdonoff, who lived down the street; he was a giant in the field of aeronautical engineering. He used to teach me how to make model airplanes and let me fly them. When something went wrong, like it crashed into a tree or it didn't take off, rather than tell me what I had done wrong he would ask me questions about what I would do differently to try to keep that from happening again.

I guess the common thread with all these people is: rather than tell me the answer, they taught me how to ask the questions. That is a gift for which I will be grateful for as long as I'm breathing.

> I'm currently working on the Pain Free Socket, a prosthetic device which incorporates the concept of thermal biofeedback into the prosthetic socket that has the potential to eliminate phantom limb pain in amputees. I invented the PFS after meeting military amputees returning from Iraq and Afghanistan, and I hope to make pain one less obstacle in their rehabilitative process.
>
> **Katherine Bomkamp** (Twice Intel International Science and Engineering Fair Winner and the CEO of Katherine Bomkamp International)

You have often made clear that you have a burning passion to help children learn to be innovative. What steps do you think need to be taken to facilitate innovation and innovative thought, and at what age do you think this should begin?

If you grow up in a household where your parent or parents are illiterate, by the time you make it to kindergarten you've heard about 1 million fewer words spoken, and the range of topics is much smaller. So you're already a year and a half or two behind your peers in straight old communication.

The next issue is in poor environments where, for instance, you don't get adequate eye testing. In countries like India and China, one out of every thousand people is so debilitated visually they are unable to take care of themselves. Between those two countries alone, you're talking about over 2 million people that are totally helpless. Sixty percent of the children in US city schools have reading problems, about half of which are simply because they can't see the letters and the words well enough. So, by the time that's detected, they're another few years behind.

We have a [US] school system, exacerbated by President Bush's 'No Child Left Behind', where we are punishing the kids who have disadvantages and not rewarding the ones who have advantages. The best analogy I can give you is the Jewish grandmother who has two chickens, one of which is sick, one of which is healthy. She kills the healthy one to make chicken soup for the sick one, to nurse it back to health. I had a big fight with Margaret Spelling when she was Secretary of Education; I called her programme: 'No Child Gets Ahead', rather than 'No Child Left Behind'.

You've spoken about how people are born with the ability to think innovatively but have that ability 'squeezed' out of them from a very young age. Do you think it's something we can remember how to do; and can one be too old to remember how?

As a matter of fact, it gets better as we get older. If you consider the world to be a giant jigsaw puzzle, every year you pick up a few new pieces for you to try to figure out how to put them together. The older you get – unless you come down with Alzheimer's or you get elected to the US Congress – you have a bigger stack of pieces that you can potentially put together.

You are working on a number of things now, all of which are incredibly interesting and have amazing potential, for instance your development of a 'silk-like' material.

I am in the thick of developing a class of fabrics which will be fireproof, waterproof and as light as silk. There are enormous opportunities ranging from construction to medical to safety. When completed I expect that thousands of lives will have been saved by my fabrics and many new jobs will have been created.

What happened was, I got a phone call from a colonel at the Pentagon who began the discussion by saying, 'You know a lot of us down here hate Dupont.' I asked him what his beef was with them and he said, 'We have been after them for 10 years to raise the melting point of nylon by just 100°, because when an IED goes off, the soldiers get injured and the fireball that results melts the nylon into their burns. The lucky ones die, the unlucky ones live. But what's really irritating is: Dupont has some cowardly executive named Newton, who won't even show up at the meetings, but claims it can't be done!'

I thought that was just a really clever joke, but no. What he was hearing was: Newton's law of thermodynamics, which says it can't be done. He didn't realize [it wasn't] an executive named Newton. I explained to him that he was asking the wrong question.

He needed a fabric similar to nylon, but one that didn't melt at the same temperature.

Correct. I made such a fabric over a weekend. It was an ah-ha moment. As a result we're forming a new company called The Fractured Forehead, because when I hear of such things, I hit myself in the head and say, 'Why didn't I think of that!' It's the umbrella for a lot of new ventures.

Such as Vaporiety and the 'Smell the coffee' technology?

Absolutely! The history of Vaporiety is: my wife adores coffee. I halfway believe if she could walk around with an IV-stand behind her, dripping coffee into her veins, she would do so.

She and our daughters have complained a thousand times that their coffee doesn't taste very good in a travel mug. Thinking about it, it was really sort of obvious… the lid that's keeping it from spilling is keeping the aroma from getting to your nose, and smell is vitally important in taste. It took me about 10 minutes to figure out how to do it. The reason I like to talk about that is because it debunks the myth that to be innovative, you have to spend $5 million or have a PhD.

> *Innovation is the craft of turning creative ideas into reality. Being creative is one thing, but innovation is the completion of generating the idea into an operational 'thing' that generates revenue, wealth and jobs, hopefully.*
> **John E Barnes** (Leader of CSIRO's Titanium Technologies Theme)

Keyword imagination exercise

Child, Mentor, Motivate, Play, Question

Vint Cerf

Photo credit:
Google/Weinberg-Clark

Vint Cerf is the co-inventor of the internet, its architecture and core TCP/IP protocols. He is Google's VP and Chief Internet Evangelist, President of the Association for Computing Machinery, former ICANN board chairman, and a Distinguished Visiting Scientist at the Jet Propulsion Laboratory, where he is working on the design and implementation of an interplanetary internet. Among his multitude of international awards and commendations, he is a recipient of the US National Medal of Technology, the ACM Alan M Turing Award (sometimes known as the 'Nobel Prize of Computer Science') and the Presidential Medal of Freedom – the highest civilian award given by the United States to its citizens. Vint was inducted in the Inventors Hall of Fame and has been awarded the Library of Congress Bicentennial Living Legend medal.

You have given us the internet and now, with your work at the Jet Propulsion Laboratory, it seems you're working on giving us the 'interstellar-net'.

I am part of a team originating at JPL but now including all NASA laboratories and other research groups that has been working on the design and implementation of a networked communication architecture for space exploration. It is especially focused on deep space communication that also must deal with more complex topologies. For example, around Mars today there are four orbiters and two operating rovers – one of which landed in January 2004 and another that landed August 5 2012.

Future missions to Mars and elsewhere will likely include distributed sensor networks, aerostats, rovers and, ultimately, astronauts. The so-called interplanetary 'Bundle Protocol' has been tested on the International Space Station, on the EPOXI spacecraft that has rendezvoused with two comets, and in prototype form on three rovers and two orbiters as well as the Earth Observation satellite (EO-1). We have discovered that the properties of the Bundle Protocol make it suitable for supporting communication in the hostile environments of military tactical, civilian mobile and public safety communication systems. It is also very useful for the support of sensor networks that may experience only intermittent connectivity. We anticipate use in civilian mobile applications during the rest of this decade and beyond.

I am also involved in a project sponsored by the Defense Advanced Research Projects Agency (DARPA) to design a spacecraft that can travel to a nearby star in 100 years elapsed time. The nearest star, Proxima Centauri, is near the binary Alpha Centauri system and it is 4.3 light years away. An Earth-like rocky planet has been discovered to be in orbit around Alpha Centauri B. There are many challenges including propulsion, navigation and communication. If our design is feasible, this could result in the development and launch of the first interstellar exploration mission.

> *I currently run a start-up called 'I Dream of Space' which aims to make space travel more accessible to the broader populace, by running a kind of draw; every time people buy a $10 poster, they get a 1 in 25,000 chance of going to space. On the surface, it's a simple mechanism to bring the unit-price below the disposable income threshold and thereby make it accessible to the masses... but behind the scenes it's a hearts and minds campaign. What we're creating is an accessible market – and demand; something the space industry desperately needs if it's going to attract serious investors into the future.*

Reuben Metcalfe (Founder of IDreamofSpace.com)

Coming back to earth, what transformational shift in IT do you think is necessary to enable users to move freely with their data?

We must invent a rich way to encode the semantics of information so as to achieve its accessibility and discoverability in the vast and growing archives of information found on the internet (and off it).

You've often spoken of the need for a 'Rosetta Stone for data' to ensure that data remains useable over time.

If we do not invent this data Rosetta Stone, [we] will be doomed to lose the work of the past – it will be worse than the dark ages.

In an earlier conversation we spoke a great deal about the need for net neutrality. Now I'd like to ask you about the freedom of the internet. Specifically, do you think that 'internet freedom' is an imperative to enable the flourishing of innovation?

Democratic societies cannot survive unless there is freedom to speak and to hear. Moreover, in this increasingly networked world, we are going to have to work very hard to achieve freedom from harm as well. There is a *lot* of work to be done to harness this distributed and networked computing environment for the benefit of all mankind.

And how important do you think innovation is to us as individuals and society as a whole?

Society cannot progress unless it is able to provide for its members to innovate. The invention of agriculture greatly increased the opportunity for innovation. It is also incredibly satisfying on an individual basis to scratch a dissatisfaction itch and discover an innovation that improves life.

> Farmers are the first innovators. For 10,000 years, ever since we domesticated crops and had agriculture, farmers have been innovating, starting from primitive seed saving and experimenting to identify seeds that produce the best yields and flavours.

Of course today, farming continues to play a critical role in human, environmental and economic health. These are some of the reasons that farmers continue to be great innovators. Whether it's a for-profit operation like farmers in the United States, or subsistence operations in less-developed countries, farmers are always looking for innovation. They are looking for new seeds with novel genetic combinations that are going to produce desirable traits such as resistance to disease and tolerance of environmental stresses. They are experimenting with new farming practices that safeguard the environment and the health of farm workers.

My laboratory is identifying genes in rice, the most important staple food for the world's people, that confer tolerance to stress and resistance to disease. Together with my collaborators at the International Rice Research Institute, we identified a rice gene that confers two weeks' tolerance to submergence. In 2012, an estimated 2 million farmers in India and Bangladesh grew this new variety, which yielded two to five-fold more grain than conventional varieties when the farmers were flooded. My husband, an organic farmer, experiments with farming methods and new seed varieties that maximize productivity while minimizing harmful inputs.

Pamela Ronald (Award-winning plant geneticist and co-author of *Tomorrow's Table: Organic farming, genetics and the future of food*)

Keyword imagination exercise

Benefit, Explore, Freedom, Future, Mankind

Fiorenzo Omenetto

Fiorenzo Omenetto is a Professor of Biomedical Engineering and leads the laboratory for Ultrafast Non-linear Optics and Biophotonics at Tufts University, where he also holds an appointment in the Department of Physics. His research interests cover optics, nanostructured materials, nanofabrication and biopolymer-based photonics. Pioneering (with David Kaplan) the use of silk as a material platform for photonics, optoelectronics and high-technology applications, and co-inventor on over 70 disclosures on the subject, Fiorenzo is actively investigating novel applications that rely on this technology base (deemed one of the top 10 technologies likely to change the world). Named one of the top-50 people in tech by *Fortune Magazine*, Fiorenzo is a former J Robert Oppenheimer Fellow at Los Alamos, a Guggenheim Fellow for 2011, and a Fellow of the Optical Society of America.

Your research is focused on interdisciplinary themes and the cross-fertilization of knowledge. Is that a smooth process?

Interdisciplinary planning doesn't make a lot of sense to me. Everybody talks about it but I think that there are certain archetypes of scientists, of artists, architects, of – I don't know… farmers – that are willing to engage without fear, and the lack of fear is important. The analogy I always give is: when you try to learn a foreign language, you're going to be successful if you're absolutely willing to make mistakes and be prepared to make a fool of yourself. If you're not willing to do that, you will never be as successful as the people that do.

The willingness to face fears – to acknowledge them, but then push past them – is a common theme in these interviews; along with giving oneself the permission to fail.

I also think you have to have a healthy dose of self-deprecation. It's also a great defence mechanism. However, not taking yourself too seriously is very different from not being serious.

And innovation can be quite serious both when innovating for science and when innovating for survival.

Yes. I live an amazingly privileged life, where I can afford to think about 'big' things. Maybe, if I had to worry about daily survival, my innovation would be more pragmatic – more directed towards a better spear for hunting.

But instead, you are working with silk. As I understand it, silk is something of a miracle material. It's sustainable, biodegradable, edible, implantable, technological. Frankly, I'm surprised it's not tap dancing! What is your big, hairy, audacious goal for it?

There are two big, hairy, audacious goals. One is related to vaccines and stabilization issues: being able to store biologicals at room temperature would be tremendous. For instance, being able to store a rotavirus vaccine at room temperature means that you're going to do a lot of good for a lot of kids that die of dysentery. [The technology would save almost half of the vaccines produced each year that are currently destroyed due to temperature difficulties.]

On the technological side, the big far-reaching goal is to think about silk as a substitute for plastic. It's very ambitious because it's still expensive; it's not economically feasible to substitute silk cups at McDonald's. But eventually we might be able to substitute sophisticated technological material (like photonics and electronics) with a silk-based material that could then degrade and reintegrate harmlessly in the environment. So, a lot of things like cell phones and electronic components that go in landfills could degrade and reintegrate in the environment. How amazing would it be if you had a compostable iPhone, right?

> *Since 2005, in collaboration with universities and organizations all over the world, we have been working toward creating the enterprise of the future, a sustainable knowledge-intensive enterprise that combines forward-looking innovation with rapid learning. This next-generation enterprise focuses on keeping its internal speed of change equal to or faster than the external speed of change in the marketplace.*
>
> *The problems and opportunities we are facing now and in the years ahead are extremely complex and fast-moving. The good news about competing in today's world is that nobody owns a monopoly on innovation. Those enterprises that can bring the full complement of their intellectual capital to bear through a continuous cycle of rapid innovation and learning will succeed. Those who do not will be rendered irrelevant.*
>
> **Art Murray** (CEO of Applied Knowledge Sciences, Inc,
> and Chief Architect of the Enterprise of the Future)

How expensive is silk to work with in comparison to other things?

Polystyrene, PVCs and plastics, in general, have been around for so long that they're processing price point is very low today. However, the chemical process that is necessary to solubilize silk fibres is a lot like making pasta. You boil against the salt, the silk fibres melt and then you remove the salt. When you dialyse the salt away you're left with water and silk – liquid silk if you will. It is a very green chemical process because you can recuperate the water that you boil with and, in principle, recuperate the salt.

I think that everything will start to come down in price; and there's nothing quite like demand to start streamlining processing and getting people to think about the innovation scaling up.

I suppose it comes down to how you count cost, whether you're counting dollars instead of making sense.

I think that's a great point. In fact the carbon footprint in this process is incredibly low.

Is there some way that the general reader can support your initiative?

Not right now. But I'm hoping that there will be. Part of the dream is to build a 'silk institute', or laboratory, to provide the materials and continue to fuel innovation in support of the applications, whether it be the stabilization of vaccines or meltable iPhones.

The potential could transform millions, if not billions of lives.

The reason that silk can 'tap dance' is that it has a lot of attributes that you can mix and match. Take any piece of plastic around your house and think: what if. What if I could eat 'that'? What if 'this' contained vitamins? What if 'that' talked to my cell phone? Suddenly your mind starts to go a little bit crazy... you start thinking: what if I could integrate it into my body!

Creative thinking... speaking of which, I understand you're a musician. What instrument do you play?

The guitar... I can shake other stuff.

A lot of the innovators I've spoken to play music. They seem to find it gives them a great release, and the potential for, if you will, 'jazz' thinking.

I think it's incredibly important to have a balance – a left brain/right-brain balance – especially in the sciences. So, the music, photography and all the art communities that I interact with, all help a tremendous amount with their different viewpoints and languages; they're another piece of the puzzle, I guess. For people that are left-brain dominant, it helps to be very much in touch with the right brain and, consequently, for people that are right-brain dominant – as long as they're willing to try to communicate.

And there is always method to the right brain. I try to convey to my students that things like music don't come easily. You can listen to the most soulful piece, seemingly so spontaneous, yet behind that spontaneity there are endless hours of repetition and mechanics.

Thelonious Monk and John Coltrane didn't just sit down and have 'it' come to them.

No. They certainly knew how to play those intervals. They were deeply in touch with their feelings and willing to bare them… and they could connect the mechanics of their fingers to their mood and their soul. They knew how to make those intervals sing.

Keyword imagination exercise

Balance, Engage, Fool, Miracle, Mistake

Michael Laine

Author and former member of the NASA Institute for Advanced Concepts research team project, Michael Laine is President and Chief Strategic Officer of the LiftPort Group which is working towards the completion of an elevator in space.

Photo: Heisenburg Media/Lift Port

Setting a goal such as you have, to build an elevator to space, is quite audacious. And one that takes a fair amount of mettle. I'd suggest that you're not afraid of failure, nor are you afraid of making mistakes. Is that something that you cultivated or is it part of your DNA?

In America, a lot of people have connections back to 'Mother England'. My mom will be the first to tell you that, somehow or another, we're related to that guy who [killed] the dragon.

St George?

George, right. We're also related to two guys I actually care about… Daniel Boone and Meriweather Lewis – of the Lewis and Clarke Expedition.

That's how I gravitate. My folks gravitate to royalty and ancient lineage and I want to know the guy who's out wrestling grizzly bears and carving a path across the country. So I do think it's in my DNA, but I also think you can cultivate it. The first thing you have to do is turn off your television. Slavish attention to somebody else's creativity is probably not the way to get there.

One of the first things I did was establish a basic vision, mission and values. That's the core to it all. Who are you? What are you trying to accomplish? Where are you trying to go? How are you going to get there? Who's going to come with you? It sets the foundation for everything.

If your foundation – your vision, mission, values – is: I am going to be innovative... then you do that. You have to choose: I am going to be innovative, I am going to be creative, I am going to push the envelope.

What have your choices cost you?

Financially, it's somewhere north of $2.5 million, but that's a fuzzy number. It's probably higher than that because of potential revenues that have been lost – that would probably bring us closer to $8–10 million; but that's even more subjective. So let's simplify and stick with $2.5 million.

Beyond financial costs, there have been personal, family and social costs. I don't want to talk about these – but they must be acknowledged.

But not everything of value is calculable financially, is it?

Exactly. In the same way that you choose creativity, you can choose your values. I vividly remember the day I decided that I could either have a building or my project. I could either pay my mortgage or I could pay my team. Up until that point the project was about wealth generation... greed. I was financially comfortable, but I wasn't rich. I thought: Hey I could be rich... I might as well do that.

But, when you make a conscious decision to pay your team and not pay your mortgage... at that moment, it stops being about wealth and it starts being about something bigger. At the time I probably didn't have the maturity to really define it, but it was the right choice.

And yes, there was a cost but the value of it... the results of it – that is incalculable. This sounds kind of corny, and it's not my style, but I think I'm a better person, a better human being now, having gone through that.

> " Innovation is an alchemy; it is a precious blend of know-how, empathy and vision to be used in unexplored territory. It is imperative to have faith, to have no fear of the future, and to understand that, often, the greatest barrier to innovation is yourself and the constraints you burden yourself with.
>
> **Jean-Sébastien Robicquet** (Founder, President, Director General and Master Distiller at EWG Spirits and Wines)

And what about the personal costs?

I've always been an all-or-nothing kind of guy. I'm 44 and it is extremely unlikely that I'm ever going to have a wife and kids. On this path, I don't see how that fits.

I am the guy who bets the mortgage. How many sane, rational women, that want to have kids and a minivan, are going to think twice about a guy who bets the mortgage? It's not to say there're not some amazing people out there. But it radically shrinks the pool.

So yes, the cost is high. I wanted kids, I wanted to marry. Now, at 44, I'm starting this new path and even I can't imagine it. How can you give a wife and child the attention they deserve and still build an elevator on the moon? I kind of let that ship sail... and I'm ok with that.

You were a Marine, and yet I note that you were branded insubordinate and a troublemaker as a schoolchild. Those might be qualities that are really useful to an innovator, but less so in the military.

I was meritoriously promoted... and I almost lost my extra stripe for exactly the same qualities. Yes, the Marine Corps did not always appreciate my perspective.

I definitely was a troublemaker, but not the class clown who was always getting attention. I wasn't the pothead [or] the bad ass kid who's got a great car and leather jacket – none of those guys were me.

I wasn't interested in going to school because I knew that I was learning more in *my* environment than I was learning in *their* environment. In three years I skipped more than 130 school days, so naturally I failed 17 classes and got suspended. I thought it was funny – I didn't want to go to school in the first place and then they go and throw me out of school for an extra six weeks! As far as I was concerned that was a big win! But there is a price you're gonna have to pay – if you are going to carve your own path.

I damn sure wasn't going to stay in school an extra year and I wasn't going to drop out. So, my junior and senior year, I'd get out of high school at 2 o'clock, jump in my car, race across town, and go to the local community college to take real classes until 7 or 9 o'clock at night. I would skip high school all the time but I damn sure didn't skip college classes. If you're going to carve your own path, you have to be aware of, and prepared for, the consequences.

As well as being a trail blazer, you're also an embodiment of the cross-fertilization of skills and experiences necessary to move your project forward. You're a gifted communicator, you have an ability to focus, and you have the imagination to envisage your dream and the processes to develop it. All of these things seem to be perfect for LiftPort.

I was lucky. Check out this quote from Robert Heinlein's *Time Enough for Love*: 'A human being should be able to change a diaper, plan an invasion, butcher a hog, conn a ship, design a building, write a sonnet, balance accounts, build a wall, set a bone, comfort the dying, take orders, give orders, cooperate, act alone, solve equations, analyse a new problem, pitch manure, program a computer, cook a tasty meal, fight efficiently, die gallantly. Specialization is for insects.'

So let me look at this list: I can change a diaper. I can plan a minor invasion, not a large one. I cannot butcher a hog; I probably would if I had to but, really, I would defer that one. I have conned a ship. I can design a small building but not a large one. I can write a haiku but not sonnets. I don't like balancing my cheque book, ask anyone, but I am able. I screwed up building a wall – I almost knocked one over and I did permanently embed my best friend's 30-year-old hunting knife in the concrete. I've broken more than 20 bones so I absolutely know how to set one.

My step-mom died a week ago this morning. A massive heart attack struck on New Year's Eve, and over the course of the next few days it was a slow, agonizing spiral down and down. I held her hand to her very last breath. I can comfort the dying. But more importantly, after more than 50 USMC burial details and after helping my family, I can say that I am better at comforting the left-living.

I can take orders, I can give orders, I can cooperate, I can act alone, I can solve minor equations… but I'm really bad at higher math. I love analysing new problems – that's my favourite.

I have pitched manure. I paid for my prom by shovelling sheep shit. But I took a helicopter to prom – I shovelled a lot of manure to do that. I dug fence posts, patched a barn roof and shovelled a lot of sheep shit. But I took a girl to my prom in a helicopter.

Wow, she will never forget that.

And her husband of 20-plus years will never forget it either…. We all knew each other in high school – she only ever had two boyfriends that mattered. More than a quarter century after we all graduated… he still doesn't like me. She *did* pick the right guy though… And I'm glad for both of them that she did.

I can't program a computer anymore but I used to be able to. I can't cook particularly well. I can fight efficiently. I have no experience in dying gallantly but I promise I won't go easily.

I didn't come up with the skills to build an elevator to space by design. How could I possibly do that? I was reading [Robert] Heinlein and [Arthur C] Clark at a pretty young age, but I couldn't have planned where I am today. No how, no way; it's impossible to plan for something like this. I'm lucky.

You say lucky, but the fact is that, when the ring came along, you jumped for it and hung on.

Yes. I am persistently at the right place at the right time; and, because I am very good at pattern recognition, I can actually plan to be at the right place at the right time. That's pretty awesome, and is a skill I've worked pretty hard to develop.

I like perseverance and tenacity. The rational side of me says: all right, just know when to quit. And then the pride in me says: quit my ass! I go all the way, for better or worse.

I think for a 'grand project' such as building a space elevator you have to go for it... there is no hedging your bets. There is no later, there is now. 'Now' is a river that keeps flowing and you've got to go on that ride; if you pull up on the bank you might miss that thing around the corner, and that could be the best thing ever.

Right! It's an interesting path I've taken, and I'm glad of it, even if there are days when it gets pretty tiring.

Speaking of interesting paths, do you think it's a good idea that you are, in essence, making a path for human beings to take to the stars? It's not like we've done the greatest job of managing our own rock.

Clearly, the answer is yes. People should be asking that question, but I'm going to flip it around and say: we've done a great job of managing this rock.

We've done the very best job that this solar system can do in managing a rock, because, we're 'it'... the only option there is. If life is going to move beyond this rock, there is only one apex predator that can do it. So if your question is: have we harmed the Earth? Absolutely, no question. But if your question is: can the one apex predator in the solar system move the rest of life beyond its borders? We're the only game in town. If it's not us, it's the dinosaurs, and they had their shot.

Yes, we have harmed our oceans, our trees and our mountains. We've harmed countless species, some of which we'll never even know existed because they became extinct before we got the ink to write about them. But, as a whole, out of the 1.5 million species that we do know of, if they're going to move beyond this one rock, if they're going to perpetuate, there's only one game in town. If you really think that life deserves to move beyond the Earth, there's only one option and that's us.

Without humanity to give it a voice, there can be no poetry on Mars. Without humanity to give it motion, there can be no dance on the Moon. Without humanity to bring cows and sheep and redwoods, then those critters are going to be confined to Earth. And Earth is a closed biosphere. It might take a while, but a closed biosphere is always doomed. So I think, if you really revere life, the only option is to go to space and take everything else with us.

Bearing in mind that you're doing something on a 'greater than global' scale; do you see the space elevator as something that is part of a common wealth of nations, or is it something that only the very wealthy will be able to participate in?

It's absolutely the common wealth of nations, but that commonwealth of nations has to pay. The robber barons that built the American railroads determined who went where, how often, and at what price. And that's what we're building… we're building the railroad in space.

We're going to have that power. But, going back to those guys, it was in their best long-term interest to make it as massively available as possible. Back then you could go from New York to San Francisco for $55. Well, even if $55 was a lot, compared to the many thousands it took to buy a wagon, a team and supplies for the journey, it was a great bargain. So that's what we're going to do: we're going to lower the bar and make it as available as possible.

Let me explain how the lunar elevator works. Imagine this: you've got an extraordinarily long, strong thread, a thin ribbon the size of dental floss. You attach this onto the surface of the Moon, with a robot we call a 'Spike'. Pull this ribbon out, through the Lagrange point and far, far back toward the Earth – so that the counterweight is relatively deep in Earth's gravity well. Earth's gravity keeps the ribbon pulled (gently) tight.

That's the construction phase. Once that's complete then we start using it. We launch from Earth in a geosynchronous rocket (there're about 30 from 14 nations), we climb to the Lagrange point space station and use the elevator to gently lower cargo and people to the surface of the Moon.

Now what would happen if Japan went to the Moon? They have a rocket that's capable of it. Could they go to the Moon in eight years? Absolutely. China is certainly going to go. What about India? How is Pakistan going to handle it? What happens when Israel and Iran go to the Moon? These are world-changing situations. This is absolutely a commonwealth of nations; but it's not going to be run by the United Nations. I think it forces us to figure out how to get along a little bit better.

Take a couple of minutes to study how it works in Antarctica. It has its own government but it's not sovereign. There are treaties, rules and methods of being; it's an amalgam of many other nations, and I think that we're going to want to use Antarctica as a map for how we operate [on the Moon]. I hope so. It's a good map.

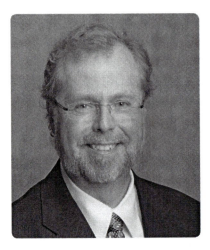

The barriers to innovation are that people are afraid of things that are new. They're afraid because they're risky – and they're not wrong, they are risky! It's much riskier to have something that's brand new and never been done before than something which has been around for a long time. So, you need an environment where it's ok to take some chances; where you're self-confident enough that you can pick yourself up if it doesn't work and dust yourself off and try again.

Dr Nathan Myhrvold (Innovator, inventor, founder of Intellectual Ventures, former Microsoft CTO and Chief Strategist, creator/co-author of Modernist Cuisine and Modernist Cuisine at Home)

Keyword imagination exercise

Cooperate, Dream, Imagine, Journey, Tenacity

SUMMARY

In the Introduction I noted that there were no right or wrong answers. This is a truism I stand by; but innovation is not a spectator sport – it is active; you have to *do* it. So ask yourself: is innovation something that happens to you, because of you, or in spite of you? If you don't like your answer, do something about it. *Do* something.

Yes, I admit that 'innovation' is a buzzword being bandied about, some might say too liberally at times, but we must beware of innovation fatigue and complacency. Though all people are not created equally innovative, we can all celebrate, support and reward it.

The ABCs of the new knowledge-based Global Digital Economy are: Agile, Borderless and Cooperation. It is organizations with flexible processes and agile structures that will be able to best take advantage of the coming innovative opportunities. As our global connections increase, borders – national, organizational or institutional – will be ever more arbitrary and irrelevant, and empowered endusers will expect to be able to access, define and refine content and information regardless of where they happen to reside.

Though data confidentiality and security should be sacrosanct, the ability to collaborate and cooperate imperative. Tools and technologies are arriving that enable simple, secure, multidisciplinary – and, as it's a flat world, multilingual – collaboration, cooperation and the cross-fertilization of ideas and knowledge. These must be embraced, as inspiration leading to innovation and innovative solutions can come from anywhere and anyone – often from the most unlikely of sources. Innovation, in one guise or another, must be part of an organization's strategic vision, mission and plan or it will be 'outsmarted' in the knowledge-based GDE.

All that said, let's not forget that innovation and innovating can be great fun. Perhaps the best exemplars of this are children who, in exploring the world for the first time, are inveterate innovators. Constantly curious, children are full of wonder: they imagine, ask why, and what if. Unafraid to touch, try, run and fall, they get back up and try again. They play – and are well aware it's much more fun to play together than to play alone.

Tag, you're it!

BIOGRAPHIES

The interviewees

A former banker and financial analyst and business development manager, **Noor Aftab** (Pakistan) is an author, speaker, business adviser and disruptive innovator. Her latest initiative is as the co-founder of the Shaina Aftab Foundation which works to transform the lives of people in need. In recognition of her work, she received the Women/ Super Achiever Award 2012 from the Asia Pacific HRM Congress.

Esra'a Al Shafei (Bahrain) is a TED Senior Fellow, founder and Director of Mideast Youth and crowdvoice.org, and an innovator in the use of digital technology and digital media for human rights activism.

Author **Debra M Amidon** (United States) is founder and CEO of ENTOVATION, a global innovation research and consulting network connecting 67 nations. Considered an original architect of the knowledge economy, she has consulted for Fortune 50 companies, universities and societal organizations (eg, the World Bank, the OECD, the UN and the IADB). As a sponsor of the World Summits on Innovation and Entrepreneurship (WSIE), her concept of knowledge innovation is a cornerstone for economic development in a multitude of countries. She is a global expert on collaborative advantage providing an innovation foundation for economic sustainability, stakeholder innovation and world peace.

Jack Andraka (United States), a 15-year-old Maryland high school student and teen trailblazer, invented an inexpensive, sensitive dipstick-like sensor for the rapid and early detection of pancreatic, ovarian and lung cancers. His research was conducted at the lab of Dr Anirban Maitra at Johns Hopkins University School of Medicine Department of Pathology in the Sol Goldman Research Institute.

Winner of the 2012 International Science Fair, Jack exemplifies young, visionary innovators. He is the youngest ever member of the global growth partnership company, Frost & Sullivan's Global Board of Advisors for GIL Global, the Global Community of Growth, Innovation and Leadership.

Scott Anthony (United States) is a Managing Partner at Innosight, Chairman of the IDEAS Ventures investment committee and a sought-after international consultant on growth and innovation. Writing extensively on the subject of innovation as an author, co-author and columnist, Scott specializes in disruptive innovation, media, telecommunications and consumer packaged goods.

Rob Atkinson (United States) is President of the Information Technology and Innovation Foundation in Washington, DC. Rob is a renowned author and thought leader in public policy, economic development as well as knowledge and innovation economics.

John E Barnes (United States/Australia) is leader of CSIRO's Titanium Technologies Theme with approximately 70 scientists and engineers specializing in titanium metal production and additive manufacturing. John has extensive experience within the aviation, defence and aerospace industry and is the holder of a number of patents and patents pending.

Co-founder of RO-BO.ru and Emociy.ru, **Yaroslav Baronov** (United Kingdom/Russia) is an entrepreneur and innovator specializing in social marketing, e-commerce and business development. With a strong background in engineering and business leadership, Yaroslav is currently aspiring to embrace major opportunities in the fast growing market of personal robotics, while improving the situation of corporate environmental responsibility in Russia. He is interested in discovering and providing commercially viable solutions for disruptive products, technologies and new technology ventures. Yaroslav was awarded The Rothwell Prize for outstanding research in the field of strategic business forecasting in 2012.

Matt Barrie (Australia) is a multi-award winning entrepreneur, technologist and lecturer. He is the founder and CEO of the world's largest outsourcing and crowdsourcing marketplace, Freelancer.com.

Entrepreneur, technology innovator and inventor **Yobie Benjamin** (United States/The Philippines) is the CTO for Citigroup and Chairman of Citigroup's GTS Development Innovation and Learning Centres. He has also been named as one of the top security professionals in the world by 20/20 and the Discovery Channel.

David Ben-Kay (United States/China) is the founder and Chairman of the Yuanfen-Flow Consulting Studio in Beijing, which brings together entrepreneurs, technologists, artists and designers. David's former career is as an attorney including acting as Microsoft's General Counsel and 'Piracy Czar' in China.

Author and internationally sought-after innovation consultant **Linda Bernardi** (United States) is a successful entrepreneur, innovator, investor and board member. Founder of StraTerra Partners, and the author of *ProVoke: Why the global culture of disruption is our only hope for innovation*, Linda is a thought leader with more than two decades of leadership in provocative innovation and strategic business development. Linda works actively with large global enterprises to bring disruption and enable large-scale innovation. She believes that to disrupt we first have to work through the five stages of resistance to disruption, paving the way towards collaborative innovation. In the process she is thrilled to see the membership of the culture of disruption and culture of innovation growing. Her passion is empowering and inspiring the hundreds of thousands of brilliant minds and souls in large companies to unleash their innovative talent, to see the impossible become possible around the globe, and to replace complacency with passion and ingenuity.

Abby Bloom (United States/Australia) is an experienced company director, public speaker and thought leader in innovation in health-care and medical devices, specializing in emerging economies, public-private partnerships, infrastructure development, health systems and finance, and biomedical engineering. She is co-founder and CEO of Acu Rate, an innovative medical device company specializing in transformational medical technology.

President of Current TV, **David Bohrman** (United States) has an extensive career that spans more than three decades. As a tele-vision and new media executive he has worked in network, cable, new and online media, collecting numerous awards including Emmy Peabody and Press Club awards. He is a globally respected thought leader who has been at the helm of some of the most innova-tive and impactful changes in news programming and special event news coverage.

Richard Boly (United States) is Director of the Office of e-Diplomacy at the US Department of State. He is a leader in transnational entre-preneurial ecosystems such as Mind the Bridge and a highly regarded supporter of international innovation and innovators.

Katherine Bomkamp (United States) was born in Plattsburgh, NY to Beth and Jeff Bomkamp. At the age of 16, after meeting injured soldiers returning from Iraq and Afghanistan, she invented a prosthetic device that has the potential to eliminate phantom limb pain in amputees. She is a two-time Intel International Science and Engineering Fair winner, one of *Glamour* magazine's 'Amazing Young Women' and Top Ten College Women of 2013, a *Popular Mechanics* magazine Breakthrough Award winner and the CEO of Katherine Bomkamp International (KBI). She is currently a junior at West Virginia University, majoring in political science and minoring in entrepreneurship.

Ethan Butson (Australia) is a prize-winning 16-year-old grammar school student who was awarded second place in the Materials and Bioengineering category of the 2012 INTEL International Science

Fair (ISEF), and first prize in the 2010 Australian National Science (BHP Billiton) Awards for his work with radiochromic film and UV radiation protection.

Macinley Butson (Australia), the 11-year-old sister of Ethan Butson, is an award winner in her own right, having won the Primary category of the BHP Billiton Science Awards for her Reflectacon 3000 project, which looks to reflect increased sunlight onto a solar panel to increase its electricity output potential. (Ethan and Macinley Butson, who both attend the Illawarra Grammar School TIGS, are the first brother and sister to win the two first-place awards in what is Australia's most prestigious student science competition.)

Juan Cano-Arribí (Spain) is the founder and CEO of Plantel, specializing in affordable innovation and innovation management tools and ideas. He has held the position of Chief Innovation Officer in several companies and lectures at the University of Valencia on innovation and strategy, objectives and the culture of innovation. He has published a book on these subjects with McGraw-Hill, in print and e-book formats.

Vincent Carbone (United States) is co-founder and COO of Brightidea. Over the past decade he has specialized in the implementation of strategic innovation programmes and is working towards the building of a global innovation grid.

Tamara Carleton, PhD (United States) is the founder and CEO of Innovation Leadership Board LLC, a global leader in the design of tools and processes that enable radical innovation. Currently, Dr Carleton serves as a Forum for Innovation Fellow at the US Chamber of Commerce Foundation and has held previous fellowships at the Foundation for Enterprise Development and the Bay Area Science and Innovation Consortium. Dr Carleton teaches organizational innovation and foresight strategy in Stanford University's School of Engineering executive education programme. Her most recent book is the *Playbook for Strategic Foresight and Innovation* (2013).

Vint Cerf (United States) is the co-inventor of the internet, its architecture and core TCP/IP protocols. He is Google's VP and Chief Internet Evangelist, President of the Association for Computing Machinery, former ICANN board chairman, and a Distinguished Visiting Scientist at the Jet Propulsion Laboratory where he is working on the design and implementation of an interplanetary internet. Among his multitude of international awards and commendations, he is a recipient of the US National Medal of Technology, the ACM Alan M Turing Award (sometimes known as the 'Nobel Prize of Computer Science') and the Presidential Medal of Freedom – the highest civilian award given by the United States to its citizens. Vint was inducted in the Inventors Hall of Fame and has been awarded the Library of Congress Bicentennial Living Legend medal.

Dr Gopal K Chopra, MD (United States/Australia/India) is the co-founder, President and CEO of pingmd, Inc, a New York City-based healthcare solutions company designed to reset and restore the relationship between patients and their physicians. Just prior to founding the company Dr Chopra was a senior investment banker in the healthcare group of Lazard Frères. He has practised as a neurosurgeon in Australia, India, Canada and the United States and held faculty appointments at Stanford University and the University of Melbourne. He is Associate Professor at the Fuqua School of Business, where he teaches the MBA Health Sector Management programme. Dr Chopra is the founder and host of Duke's Consumer and Wireless Healthcare conference.

Peter Cochrane (United Kingdom) is an adviser and consultant to governments and companies. He has worked across circuit, system, and network design; software, human interfaces and programming; adaptive systems; AI and AL; company transformation and management. Peter was formerly CTO BT and has also been the Collier Chair for the Public Understanding of Science & Technology at Bristol, a visiting Professor to CNET, Southampton, Nottingham Trent, Robert Gordon's, Kent, Essex and University College London. He has received numerous awards, including the C&G Prince Philip

Medal, the IEEE Millennium Medal, an OBE, the Queen's Award for Innovation and The Martlesham Medal.

Jonathan Cousins (United States) is co-founder of Cousins & Sears Creative Technologists. He is a designer, programmer and entrepreneur specializing in the creation of data visualizations, large-screen computational art, creative digital workflows and general software applications. His innovative work has been presented at various conferences and festivals, including the Sundance Film Festival.

Philippe De Ridder (Belgium) is the founder of Board of Innovation. He specializes in business development, international business models and the development of innovative, next-generation products and services.

Claire Diaz-Ortiz (United States) is an author and speaker who leads social innovation at Twitter, Inc. Named one of the 100 Most Creative People in Business by Fast Company, she recently wrote *Twitter for Good: Change the world, one tweet at a time*, her second book. She frequently speaks internationally on business and social innovation and is known for developing the TWEET model – a framework to help organizations and individuals excel on Twitter. Claire holds an MBA from Oxford University, where she was a Skoll Foundation Scholar for Social Entrepreneurship, and a BA and an MA from Stanford University. She is the co-founder of Hope Runs, a non-profit organization operating in AIDS orphanages in Kenya, and owns Interwebs Publishing. Find her via @claire on Twitter, or at www.ClaireDiazOrtiz.com.

Specializing in mechanics, automation, robotics and manufacturing automatic machines, **Enrico Dini** (Italy/United Kingdom) is immersed in developing D-Shape, 3D printing building technology to bring innovation to the architecture and construction industries.

Dr David Ferrucci, PhD (United States) is an IBM Fellow, Vice President and the principal investigator on the DeepQA (Jeopardy!-winning 'Watson') Project. He has been at IBM's T J Watson's

Research Center since 1995 where he leads the Semantic Analysis and Integration department. With over 25 patents and published papers and over 50 keynote presentations, many in highly distinguished venues, Dr Ferrucci has won multiple awards for his work on Watson and endeavours to leverage what he has learnt to drive rapid innovation in AI systems.

Matt Flannery (United States) is the CEO and co-founder of Kiva, which uses innovation in technology and micro finance to work towards the alleviation of poverty. He is a recipient of *The Economist*'s No Boundaries Innovation Award.

Founder, CEO and Chief Marketing Officer of the Social Media Group, **Maggie Fox** (Canada) is a renowned thought leader in social media and digital marketing and has been named one of Canada's Top Innovators, specializing in leadership and strategic business innovation.

Karen Freidt (United States) is Lead for the Navigation Center for Creativity, Collaboration & Innovation at the NASA Langley Research Center in Hampton, VA. With a BFA in graphic design and experience in advertising, Karen brings a creative perspective to her work leading a small team of passionate people within NASA. This innovative organization specializes in moving minds and ideas forward while piloting new ways of working within government in support of the NASA vision.

Managing Partner of Michael Johnson Associates, **Kris Gale** (Australia) has more than 25 years' experience in providing sought-after advice on Australian Federal Government programmes that support innovation and is a founding member of the Australian Federal Government's R&D Tax Incentive National Reference Group.

James Gardiner (Australia) is Lead of Design Innovation with Laing O'Rourke's Engineering Excellence Group. He is globally renowned as a thought leader in innovative construction techniques, including construction 3D printing (additive manufacturing for construction).

Adam Glick (United States) is president of The Jack Parker Corporation and a managing director at the hedge fund Tesuji Partners. An author and playwright, Mr Glick is the President and co-founder of The Floating University.

Seth Godin (United States) has written 14 bestselling books that have been translated into more than 30 languages. Deemed 'America's Greatest Marketer', he is the writer of one of the most popular blogs on the net. His Kickstarter campaign for his latest book, *The Icarus Deception*, broke records for its size and the speed that it reached its goal. Seth has founded dozens of companies, most of which failed. However, Yoyodyne, his first internet company, which was acquired by Yahoo! in 1998, pioneered permission (online) marketing. His latest company, Squidoo.com, raises money for charity and pays royalties to its million-plus members.

Lizbeth Goodman (United Kingdom/United States) is Professor of Inclusive Design and Chair of Creative Technology Innovation at University College Dublin and board member at the Innovation Academy. Founder and Director of SMARTlab and Director of Research at Futurelab Education, Lizbeth has won numerous international accolades including the Blackberry Outstanding Woman in Technology and the Microsoft Innovation in Education Award. She is a sought-after researcher, writer, presenter, performer and thought leader in a wide range of fields including arts/media programming and body language engineering interfaces for rehabilitation.

Nicholas Gruen (Australia) is the Chairman of the Australian Centre for Social Innovation. Author and speaker, he is a thought leader on information, innovation and Gov. 2.0.

Dominique Guinard (Switzerland) is a computer scientist, and the CTO/co-founder of Evrythng and WebofThings.org, which envisage an internet where every object in the world is connected via a real-time presence on the web.

Scott Heiferman (United States) is co-founder and CEO of Meetup, which is used by millions of people in over 100 countries, with over 50,000 Meetups happening each week. Meetup's new platform for mass mobilizing, 'Meetup Everywhere', is used by Oprah, *The Huffington Post*, Mashable, Etsy and others. Previously, Scott co-founded Fotolog, a photo-sharing network where over 30 million people, mostly in South America, have uploaded nearly a billion photos. He also founded i-traffic, a top online ad agency in the 1990s. An active angel investor, Scott has received the Jane Addams Award from the National Conference on Citizenship and was named the 2004 MIT Technology Review 'Innovator of the Year'.

Founder and Chair of World With No Borders, **Ebrahim Hemmatnia** (The Netherlands) is the Founder of the WillPowered Foundation, which is committed to delivering innovation and sustained international development through connecting, inspiring and empowering individuals as well as communities. In 2013 he is travelling around the world (over 35,000 miles over water and 15,000 of land), following the Equator, in one vehicle, the BootFiets – the world's first amphibian and pedal-powered boat!

At 24, **Tony Hsieh** (United States) sold LinkExchange, the company he co-founded, to Microsoft for $265 million. He then joined online shoe and clothing store Zappos, where he eventually became CEO, and which he grew from almost no sales to over $1 billion in gross sales, annually. Zappos was purchased by Amazon in 2009 for $1.2 billion. The bestselling author of *Delivering Happiness*, which explores his entrepreneurial endeavours – and which debuted at number one on the *New York Times* Bestseller list – Tony is a committed instigator of innovation and the initiator of Las Vegas' transformational Downtown Project.

Speaker, author and award-winning entrepreneur and influencer **Tara Hunt** (Canada) is founder and CEO of the innovative online retail site, Buyosphere.

Renowned speaker, strategist and entrepreneur, **Salim Ismail** (Canada) is co-founder, Executive Director and Global Ambassador for the Singularity University and Chairman of Confabb. Formerly VP at Yahoo, Salim has founded or operated seven early-stage companies that were instrumental in some of the foundational technology for the real-time web. Multi-award winning, Salim is a thought leader in the future of the internet, digital media, entrepreneurship and private equity.

Robert Jacobson (United States) is CEO, co-founder, Chairman and Strategist at Atelier Tomorrow based in both San Francisco and Malmö, Sweden. A lifelong student of human experience, Robert is an expert on innovation-management issues, especially the development of regional innovation platforms that produce continuous social and technological innovation.

Founder of the Move India Foundation, **Dr Sridhar Jagannathan** (United States/India) is Chief Innovation Officer at Persistent Systems, a global software engineering company. His career has seen him in positions such as ocean engineer, entrepreneur, venture capitalist, technologist and innovator. Sri specializes in technology innovation, business strategy and entrepreneurship.

Dominique Jaurola (Australia/Finland) is a business designer, product creator, futurist, intrapreneur and entrepreneur. She has brought about change in human-centricity, mobile (consumer and enterprise) and the connected world over the last 20 years. In a global product leader role at Nokia she shaped the nascent digital and mass-market mobile world in the mid-1990s. Hunome, her second start-up, is a web application akin to genome but instead of mapping DNA, it connects and contextualizes shared perspectives into mind-maps for better access to human-centric knowledge.

Linda Jenkinson (United States) is Chairman and co-founder of LesConsierges Inc. She is a sought-after keynote speaker, successful serial entrepreneur, global strategist, expert and innovative social change agent and a passionate supporter of women's empowerment through initiatives such as WOW Investments, which focuses on building women-led SMEs in West Africa.

Mary Lou Jepsen (United States) is CEO and founder of Pixel Qi. Former CTO of One Laptop per Child and Faculty Member at the MIT Media Lab, she is a renowned technology leader specializing in innovative technology management. She has been named one of *Time Magazine's* most influential people in the world, one of the top 50 Women Computer Scientists of All Time, one of the most influential people in mobile computing, and World Technology Award winner for hardware innovation, amongst other accolades.

President of InformationArchitected.com and co-founder of Level 50 Software (L50sw.com), **Dan Keldsen** (United States) is a renowned thought leader in the fields of enterprise, web and marketing 2.0, information management and architecture, innovation, collaboration and the intersection of human behaviour and digital tools.

Renowned both nationally and internationally, **Tom Kerridge** began his culinary career at 18. Moving to London he garnered experience in illustrious restaurants such as Odettes, Rhodes in the Square, Stephen Bull and The Capital. Awarded his first Michelin star in 2005 for his work at Adlards in Norwich and opening the Hand & Flowers in Marlow, with his wife Beth that same year, Tom has innovated the concept of 'gastro-pub' to something sublime. Within 12 months Tom received a Michelin star, three AA Rosettes and one Egon Ronay Star. In 2012 the Hand & Flowers became the first pub in the world to receive two Michelin stars.

Rob van Kranenburg (Belgium) wrote The *Internet of Things*, a critique of ambient technology and the all-seeing network of RFID, Network Notebooks 02 and Institute of Network Cultures. He is co-founder of bricolabs and the founder of Council. Together with Christian Nold he published *Situated Technologies Pamphlets 8: The internet of people for a post-oil world*.

Author and former member of the NASA Institute for Advanced Concepts research team project, **Michael Laine** (United States) is President and Chief Strategic Officer of the LiftPort Group, which is working towards the completion of an elevator in space.

J D Lasica (United States) is founder of the United States-based consultancies Socialmedia.biz and Socialbrite. He is a social media strategist and thought leader, entrepreneur, technology innovator, change agent, author and sought-after keynote speaker. J D has been named one of Silicon Valley's top 40 influencers, one of the top 100 influencers in social media and one of CNET's Top 100 Media Bloggers.

Jeff Leitner (United States) is the founder and Dean of Insight Labs, a foundation which brings together thought leaders to solve intractable international problems for the common good. Speaker, author and advisory board member, Jeff's former career was in public affairs, journalism and social work.

Gerd Leonhard (Switzerland) is a renowned futurist and author, provocative keynote speaker, think-tank leader and adviser, and international thought leader in topics as varied as digital business models, social media, consumer trends, entrepreneurship, branding, copyright advertising and IP protection.

Internationally renowned entrepreneur, philanthropist, diplomat, speaker and author, **Bill Liao** (Australia/Switzerland) is a venture partner with SOSventures, co-founder of the social network service XING and founder of the non-profit organization WeForest.com and co-founder of CoderDojo.

Zern Liew (Australia) juggles a lively combination of design, analysis and people skills to unravel complexity, enable light bulb moments, find ways through chaos, and turn ideas into truly useful (and beautiful) things. He has worked internationally on diverse projects across business processes, software applications and communications.

Finland's Minister of Communication from 2007 to 2011, Minister of Culture from 1999 to 2002 and a Member of Parliament from 1995 to 2011, **Suvi Linden** (Finland) is Commissioner of the United Nations Broadband Commission for Digital Development and ITU's Special Envoy for the Commission. She was nominated Visionary of the Year by Intelligent Community Forum 2011 and is founder and CEO of Pearlcon Ltd.

Jean Christophe (Chris) Lonchampt (France/Australia) is a board member at DesignGov, the Australian federal government's centre for excellence in public sector design, collaborating with the founding team and government's Secretaries, and he is the founder of Ask Sherpa. Chris sources and coaches highly innovative technology and internet projects as well as advising leaders on strategic business development and innovation culture worldwide. Chris worked and lived with his wife and three children around the world; he is a certified ski instructor and an alumnus of The Wharton School, University of Pennsylvania, Italy's Bocconi School of Management and PolytechOrleans in France.

Julian Keith Loren (United States) is an award-winning innovator who has been building design and innovation teams and taking on large-scale, multi-faceted design challenges for over 20 years. Harnessing the power of gameplay to bridge disciplines and break communication barriers, Julian designs and facilitates Gameferences – unforgettable face-to-face games that drive deep exploration and breakaway design. He is the co-founder of the Innovation Management Institute where he has helped clients such as General Electric, Johnson & Johnson, eBay and the Institute for the Future with key innovation initiatives. Julian has also lectured and run collaborative design games at Stanford University and the University of California, Berkeley and occasionally writes about technology and innovation topics.

Larry MacDonald (United States) is the CEO and founder of Edison Innovations, Inc. He is known as an innovation visionary specializing in identifying and developing solutions for new markets. His current focus is on changing children's education via KidsTeachingKids.org and changing the selection and development of new products via Edison Innovation Inc.

Co-founder and CTO of KimmiC, **Michael McDonald** (Australia) has vast experience in technological and organizational innovation, specializing in organizational growth and operational performance through innovation, communication and organization. He is a world leader in combining technology to meet need; this includes persistence through middleware through user interface, including utilizing semantic web, Java Enterprise, html5/Ajax and REST-based architecture. Michael's cross-functional capabilities include in-depth, multinational business experience through to designing, building, implementing and supporting systems along with extensive cross-cultural team-building experience. He's the creator of FlatWorld, an innovative, cross-selling, collaborative platform for cooperative knowledge management; interactive, intelligent data; and individually targeted information.

Christopher Macrae (United Kingdom) is an author, multi-award winner and global thought leader in the fields of sustainable investment and economics, networking society, knowledge collaboration and branding. He helped his father, Norman Macrae, research entrepreneurial revolution projects at *The Economist* from 1972, when they shared the life-changing moment of seeing 500 youths sharing knowledge around an early digital network. His current passion is MOOC. Generations of Chris's family have shared the International Scottish search for pro-youth economics – a worldwide curriculum likely to explain whether networked generations design futures around what 99 percent of people need most, instead of Orwell's 'Big Brother endgame'.

Founder and Head of Creative Culture at Ideafarms, **Sunil Malhotra** (India) is a thought leader in innovative outsourcing, design strategy, and 'experiential aesthetics' in the digital domain. He believes that disruptive thinking is the key business differentiator in the globalized world and works towards a paradigm of human enrichment shaped by the capabilities enshrined in borderless collaboration. He has drawn on Eastern philosophies – simplicity, inclusion and local rele-vance – to create a unique brand of innovation for socio-cultural transformation.

Amy Jo Martin (United States) is the founder and CEO of Digital Royalty. As the *New York Times* bestselling author of *Renegades Write the Rules* and member of the St Jude Digital Board of Directors, Amy Jo is a sought-after international keynote speaker on innovation in social media, personal branding and monetizing social platforms. Digital Royalty provides customized social media education pro-grammes through the Digital Royalty University, which offers a comprehensive curriculum blending strategic and tactical training. She is a regular contributor to the *Harvard Business Review, The Huf-fington Post* and *Sports Business Journal*. Follow her on Twitter @AmyJoMartin.

Dan Mathieson (Canada) has been Mayor of Stratford, Ontario since 2003. Under his leadership the city has become a leading light in the Smart Cities movement and in 2012 was designated a Top 7 Intelligent Community by the Intelligent Community Forum for the second time.

Specializing in business development and strategic partnerships, innovative boot-strapper **Reuben Metcalfe** (United States/New Zealand) is taking on the challenge of democratizing space travel through his organization IDreamofSpace.com.

Art Murray (United States) is CEO of Applied Knowledge Sciences, Inc and Chief Architect of the Enterprise of the Future. He is an ac-claimed expert and thought leader on the information economy, knowledge sharing and flat world competition. Art is Chief Fellow of the George Washington University Institute for Knowledge and Innovation, co-founding Director of its Enterprise of the Future Program and International Expert in Knowledge and Innovation Management at Bangkok University. He is a sought-after keynote speaker and editorial board member and reviewer for several scien-tific journals.

Multi-awarding winning author, innovator, inventor and the holder of hundreds of patents – and with hundreds more patents pending – **Dr Nathan Myhrvold** (United States) founded Intellectual Ventures following his retirement as CTO and Chief Strategist at Microsoft Corporation. A postdoctoral fellow in the department of applied mathematics and theoretical physics at Cambridge University, Nathan worked with Professor Stephen Hawking, earned a doctorate in theoretical and mathematical physics, a Master's degree in mathematical economics from Princeton University, and has a Master's degree in geophysics, space physics and a Bachelor's degree in mathematics from UCLA. A James Beard Award winner, Nathan is the creator and co-author of the award-winning cookbook *Modernist Cuisine* and its follow-up *Modernist Cuisine at Home*, both of which explore the application of innovative tools and techniques to the culinary arts.

Stylianos Mystakidis (Greece) is an internationally award-winning thought leader in, and designer, developer and facilitator of, e-learning and virtual immersive environments. He is a champion of educational technology, innovation and blended learning.

Nitten Nair (United Arab Emirates) is a digital and social media strategist who specializes in the linking of innovation and inspiration that can be traced back to Indian mythology.

Bill O'Connor (United States) is the founder of the Innovation Genome Project, an initiative at Autodesk that is researching the top 1,000 innovations in world history with a view to extrapolating patterns and insights that can be applied today. He works in Autodesk's Corporate Strategy team and is the primary speechwriter for the company's CEO and CTO.

SVP and Marketing Director at Author Solutions and executive responsible for bringing Booktango to market, **Keith Ogorek** (United States) is an author, sought-after speaker and well-respected thought leader in the indie publishing industry.

Fiorenzo Omenetto (United States/Italy) is a Professor of Biomedical Engineering and leads the laboratory for Ultrafast Nonlinear Optics and Biophotonics at Tufts University, where he also holds an appointment in the Department of Physics. His research interests cover optics, nanostructured materials, nanofabrication and biopolymer-based photonics. Pioneering (with David Kaplan) the use of silk as a material platform for photonics, optoelectronics and high-technology applications, and co-inventor of over 70 disclosures on the subject, Fiorenzo is actively investigating novel applications that rely on this technology base (deemed one of the top 10 technologies likely to change the world). Named one of the top-50 people in tech by *Fortune Magazine*, Fiorenzo is a former J Robert Oppenheimer Fellow at Los Alamos, a Guggenheim Fellow for 2011 and a Fellow of the Optical Society of America.

Tiago Peixoto (Brazil) is a world-renowned expert on digital democracy specializing in online participatory budgeting and wiki-legislation. An open government specialist in the ICT4Gov program of the World Bank Institute's Open Governance cluster, Tiago has worked as a policy adviser for organizations such as the OECD, the UN, and the Brazilian and United Kingdom governments, and has been involved in pioneering e-Gov initiatives in Africa, Asia, Europe, Latin America and the Caribbean. Among other publications, Tiago is co-author of the 2010 United Nations e-government survey: *Leveraging e-Government at a Time of Financial and Economic Crisis*; he is also research coordinator of the Electronic Democracy Centre in Zurich.

Dr David Pensak (United States) is a world-renowned innovator and entrepreneur. His career includes 30 years at Dupont, from which he retired in 2004 as Chief Computer Scientist. The inventor of the world's first business firewall, the Raptor System, which was bought by AXENT Technologies (now Symantec), David's innovative entrepreneurship and leadership continues with the Pensak Innovation Institute, his authorship of *Innovation for Underdogs*, and his work for the Centre for Interdisciplinary Innovation. He is currently on the faculty of the George Washington University School of Law, the

University of Delaware Business School and is Professor of Anaesthesiology at Drexel University College of Medicine.

Jeff Power is a strategic innovator who works to enable and empower innovators, entrepreneurs and individuals in the Majority World. He does this through his work with the non-profit Global Hope Network and through Pangeo Coffee, a socially driven, for-profit organization, which Jeff founded in 2011.

Gustav Praekelt (South Africa) is the founder and CEO of the Praekelt Group and the Praekelt Foundation. He is a thought leader in the fields of mobile platforms, technology services and solutions for Majority World initiatives that have reached over 50 million people across 15 African countries.

CEO of Sparked.com, **Ben Rigby** (United States) is renowned in the fields of web and mobile product development, agile methodologies and crowdsourcing.

Emily Riley (United States) is a Connected Innovation Catalyst for General Mills Worldwide Innovation Network. She specializes in open and collaborative innovation, innovation processes and innovation opportunity strategies with core capabilities including chemical, food and beverage, fibre and renewable resources, national security, defence and education.

Founder, President, Director General and Master Distiller at EWG, Spirits and Wines, (home of the CIROC Vodka and the G'vine Gin and Cognac brands), **Jean-Sébastien Robicquet** (France) is committed to the production of ultra-premium products. Possessing generations of oenological knowledge and a deep deference for the traditions of his industry, Jean-Sébastien was awarded the title Commander of Bordeaux in acknowledgment of his 'defence and glorification of the Bordeaux wines'. His exceptional knowledge, combined with his passion for innovation, exemplifies the spirit of EWG which, with Jean-Sébastien at the helm, looks to position itself as one of the world's most innovative wine and spirits organizations.

Professor Pamela Ronald (United States) is an award-winning plant geneticist. Her laboratory has engineered rice for resistance to diseases and tolerance to flooding. Ronald was selected as one of the 100 most creative people in business by *Fast Company Magazine* and was awarded the Louis Malassis International Scientific Prize for Agriculture and Food and the Tech Award 2012 for innovative use of technology to benefit humanity. She is co-author of *Tomorrow's Table: Organic farming, genetics and the future of food*, which was selected as one of the 25 most powerful and influential books; Bill Gates called the book 'a fantastic piece of work'.

William Saito (Japan) is the founder and CEO at Intercur, KK, a bestselling author, renowned technologist and entrepreneur. Named one of the 100 most influential people for Japan, he specializes in innovative technologies and consults extensively with national governments, public/private and non-profit organizations. He is a sought-after lecturer and a Foundation Board Member at the World Economic Forum.

Engineer, designer, inventor and Managing Director of MAS Design Products Ltd, **Mark Sanders** (United Kingdom) trained as a mechanical engineer at Imperial College London and Rolls-Royce. After working in the engineering industry for several years, he also trained as a designer at the Royal College of Art in London. This combination of science and art usually gives efficient, elegant product solutions (engineering) that are also appealing and straightforward for all users (design). Mark has combined these professions for 25 years as an engineer, inventor and design consultant. His award-winning products sell in tens of millions, globally. He is a visiting lecturer at various schools and colleges in the United Kingdom and abroad, including the RCA and Imperial College.

Author, adventurer, internationally sought-after keynote speaker and environmental campaigner, **Roz Savage** (United Kingdom) holds four world records for ocean rowing, including first woman to row solo across the Atlantic, Pacific and Indian Oceans. Roz has been named a UN Climate Hero, a Fellow of the Royal Geographical

Society, Fellow of the Explorers Club of New York, one of the Top 20 Great British Adventurers, National Geographic Society Adventurer of the Year for 2010 and a Yale World Fellow.

David Schafran (United States) is Co-Founder and CEO of EyeNetra.com and an entrepreneur. With his innovative initiatives he looks to have a positive impact on the health and welfare of billions of people around the world.

David Moinina Sengeh (Sierra Leone/United States) is a graduate student and PhD candidate at MIT (MIT Media Lab) specializing in biomechatronics. Born in Sierra Leone, in 2004 David won a two-year scholarship to study at the Red Cross Nordic United World College in Norway. After completing his International Baccalaureate diploma, he enrolled at Harvard University gaining a degree in biomedical engineering. David is the Co-Founder of many organizations and social initiatives such as Global Minimum and Lebone – a team from Harvard that won a $200,000 grant from the World Bank to 'light up Africa' using microbial fuel cell technology.

Kunal Shah (India) is Founder and CEO of FreeCharge.in (brand under Accelyst Solutions Pvt Ltd), a unique and innovative business model that has revolutionized the online recharge industry. The business model is based on giving 100 percent value back to the customers who recharge their mobile phone/DTH/DataCard by providing equal-value coupons from some of the best brands, such as McDonald's, Cafe Coffee Day, Dominos, Big Cinemas, etc for free. His keen customer insight-driven business model is one of its kind across the world, which makes recharging a truly rewarding experience.

Simon Sheikh (Australia) was the National Director of GetUP, Australia's leading, online political advocacy organization from 2008 to 2012. He is running for the Australian Senate, representing the Greens Party, in the 2013 federal election.

Tiffany Shlain (United States) is a multi-award winning filmmaker, sought-after keynote speaker, prolific writer, founder of The Webby Awards and co-founder of the International Academy of Digital Arts and Sciences. Unsurprisingly, *Newsweek* named her one of the 'Women Shaping the 21st Century'. Founder of the film studio and lab The Moxie Institute, Tiffany was honoured with a 2012 Disruptive Innovation Award from The Tribeca Film Festival. Her latest innovative initiative is collaborative filmmaking, which she has termed 'Cloud Filmmaking'. A member of numerous advisory boards, an artist, advocate and activist, Tiffany's international influence is tremendous with her talks and films having been viewed over a million times.

Cecily Sommers (United States) is the author of *Think Like a Futurist: Know what changes, what doesn't, and what's next*, and the founder of The Push Institute, a non-profit think tank that tracks significant global trends and their implications for business, government and non-profit sectors over the next 5 to 50 years. Cecily's straightforward and practical approach to strategy and innovation is sought by Fortune 100 and public organizations alike. She is a member of the Association of Professional Futurists, was named by the *Business Journal* as one of 25 'Women to Watch' and Fast Company's 'Fast 50 Reader's Favorites'.

An aerospace engineer by training, **William (Bill) Storage** (United States) is a thought leader and innovator in software architecture, systems engineering and design strategy. He is a sought-after and successful CTO, entrepreneur, speaker, teacher, historian and cave explorer. As well as being an avid photographer, he is a major innovator in photographic lighting and equipment, which is brought to the fore in his work in areas such as archaeological sites and the world's deepest caves. He is a Visiting Scholar at the Center for Science, Technology, Medicine & Society at the University of California, Berkeley.

Brianna Sylver (United States) is a specialist in consumer insights and a thought leader in innovation strategy, design planning and ethnographic research. She is Founder and President of Sylver Consulting, LLC and an Adjunct Faculty Professor at the Institute of Design, IIT.

Craig Thomler (Australia) is Managing Director of Delib Australia and a Gov 2.0 thought leader. Craig has been named one of 'The 10 who are changing the face of politics and the internet' by PoliticsOnline and World e.Gov Forum.

Khayyam Wakil (United States) likes to build plans, apps, hype, strategy, products, transformational gaming, platforms, launches, start-ups, campaigns, partnerships and Lego. Loves to overcome seemingly impossible challenges in the most engaging, effective and magically unexpected ways probable with as little as possible. Loves the underdog, start-ups and the movie *Rudy*, Khayyam has made a plethora of people and companies smile by providing ideas that communicated their desired results. A man of many hats: designer, wordsmith, creative director, digital strategist, entrepreneur, marketer, business developer and most importantly, student of failure, Khayyam is currently venturing into the unknown fully willing to make mistakes and loving every minute of it.

Australian Laureate Fellow, Executive Research Director at the ARC Centre of Excellence for Electromaterials Science, and Director of the Intelligent Polymer Research Institute at the University of Wollongong, **Professor Gordon Wallace** (Australia/Ireland) is a multi-award winning thought leader in the fields of electromaterials and intelligent polymers. His specialities include organic conductors, nanomaterials, additive fabrication and electrochemical probe methods of analysis, along with the use of these in the development of intelligent polymer systems. His focus is on the use of these tools and materials in bio-communications to improve human performance via medical bionics.

Deputy Director/CIO at the World Food Programme, **Pierre Guillaume Wielezynski** (France/United States) is a sought-after public speaker and thought leader in digital strategy, marketing, social media and product development.

A thought leader in digital innovation, **Peter Williams** (Australia) started working with internet technologies in 1993 and, in 1996, founded an e-business consulting group within Deloitte Australia. Since then Peter has been CEO of the Eclipse Group and founded Deloitte Digital, which pioneered the delivery of professional services online. Chairman of Deloitte's Innovation Council since 2004, he is a sought-after speaker and commentator, locally and internationally. Peter leads the newly formed Australian Centre for the Edge Chapter, chaired by John Hagel III and John Seely Brown, which identifies and explores emerging opportunities. Named as one of Australia's top Digital Influencers, Peter is also Adjunct Professor at RMIT and a Circus Oz board member.

Faris Yakob (United States) is an award-winning strategist and creative director, writer, public speaker and geek. Most recently he was Chief Innovation Officer of MDC Partners where he founded creative technology boutique Spies&Assassins. Previously, he was Chief Digital Officer at McCann Erickson NY, and Global Digital Strategy and Creative Director at Naked Communications. He's won and judged numerous awards, strategic and creative, served as chairman of the Content&Contact and Integrated juries for the Clios, created the NEW category for the London International Awards, and teaches at Miami Ad School. Named one of the top 50 creatives in the world by the Clios, and one of 10 modern day Madmen by Fast Company, Faris' blog was named one of the top 10 blogs to follow by Mashable. He writes and speaks on technology, media, brands and creativity all over the world, and was featured in 'The Greatest Movie Ever Sold'. If you want him to write, speak, think about things or have ideas for you, @faris and farisyakob.com are where you can usually find him loitering.

Atsufumi Yokoi (Japan) is co-founder and President of Akira Foundation. He works to develop educational programmes and scholarships on social innovation and entrepreneurship for young leaders to tackle pressing issues for sustainability on the planet. Atsufumi is a Visiting International Researcher at the University of Cape Town's African Centre for Cities, where his main interest is slum upgrading for the urban poor. Atsufumi is an alumnus at the University of Cambridge's Programme for Sustainability Leadership (CPSL), and holds an MSc at the Delft University of Technology. The Akira Foundation is a strategic partner at the World Summit on Innovation & Entrepreneurship.

Hirofumi Yokoi (Japan) is co-founder (along with his twin brother Atsufumi) and President of the Akira Foundation. He specializes in developing business practices, educational programmes, social innovation and entrepreneurship. Prior to founding the Akira Foundation, Hirofumi worked with the Abdul Latif Jameel Foundation in Beirut, where he was in charge of market research and analytic solutions for social business programmes, including the Grameen-Jameel microfinance joint venture and MIT Enterprise Forum Arab Business Plan Competition. Hirofumi is a sought-after business analyst and adviser to several international social enterprises.

INDEX

CPSIA information can be obtained at www.ICGtesting.com
Printed in the USA
BVOW04s0105020813

327428BV00002B/2/P